"Rachel's book beautifully encourages me to pray; to hear, listen intently to God's Word, and then articulate the crux of the matters of the heart through written prayers. In a short amount of time, a few minutes, which is all we think we have, this devotional gives rich insights to ponder, to put into practice, and most importantly to PRAY!"

—**Kim Bolton**, Servant Heart Ministries

"Profound, real, and full of Scripture pearls! It was a treat to my soul to read *Pray Naturally*. My Spirit was being stirred as I read, reflected, and prayed back these honest and earnest prayers."

—**Sarah Breuel**, director, Revive Europe; board of directors, Lausanne Movement

"This book clearly invites women to know God's heart and kindness, and for them to share their hearts with Him too."

—**Robyn Dykstra**, speaker and author, *The Widow Wore Pink*

"All the way through, while reading about our Old Testament sisters, as Rachel took the most intimate parts of their lives and made them mine, I found myself wide-eyed by the details. The insight. And then among the final pages (day 118), I read a single line that I felt she wrote just for me. . . . As a woman whom God has placed in a position of authority, I truly *needed* that line. There is no doubt you will find your special line(s), too."

—**Eva Marie Everson**, CEO, Word Weavers International, Inc.

"Rachel Britton has gifted the reader with a treasure trove of intrigue and insights into the lives of biblical women. These women will become your sisters, Rachel's prayers will nestle in your heart, and her thoughtful questions will spur you on in your faith journey. I love this book and I know you will too."

—**Rev. Dr. Cynthia Fantasia**, speaker and author, *In the Lingering Light*

"Filled with uplifting reflections, *Pray Naturally* resonates with relatable encouragements and profound insights as the reader is guided through moments of personal introspection and spiritual growth. A must-read for anyone seeking to deepen their connection with God and find inspiration and courage in their daily lives."

—**Danielle Ievar̴···** ·or, Hillsong East Coast

PRAY NATURALLY

Finding Your Spiritual Confidence as a Woman Loved by God

RACHEL BRITTON

Our Daily Bread
Publishing.

Published in association with Books & Such Literary Management, 52 Mission Circle, Suite 122, PMB 170, Santa Rosa, CA 95409-5370, www.booksandsuch.com.

Interior design by Michael J. Williams

ISBN: 978-1-64070-368-1

Library of Congress Cataloging-in-Publication Data Available

Printed in the United States of America
25 26 27 28 29 30 31 32 / 8 7 6 5 4 3 2 1

Dedicated to my grandmother, Beatrice Maude Beales,
and my mother, Patricia Elizabeth Mullender,
who modeled for me the beauty of prayer.

CONTENTS

Contents

Contents

Contents

A woman with purpose: Practicing prayer from the life of Esther

INTRODUCTION

God wants you to talk with Him and trust in Him.

Prayer is that simple. Did you let those words sink in? The God who hangs the stars in place and names each of them longs for you to spend time with Him. He says, "_____ (insert your name), talk to Me and trust Me." Close your eyes for a moment and repeat those words. God is saying them to you. Does that request stir your heart? Or does your heart sink? Maybe you feel you're no good at talking with God. Maybe you find it hard to completely trust God. Do you immediately answer back with a but? "But, I can't . . ." "But, I don't . . ." "But, I find . . ."

I also struggle with being confident in prayer and being fully assured God has got me, especially when things aren't going well. But, in the middle of my wrestling to pray and know God well, when I hear "Rachel, talk to Me and trust Me," my heart misses a beat. You know that feeling when you realize someone likes you a lot, or even loves you? The delightful surprise that you are special—or maybe you had hoped, but now you're sure. And, the realization that, yes, God is trustworthy, more than anything or anyone else in your life.

We want our knees to go weak when God woos us with "Talk to Me." God's love for us should make our legs buckle, because weak knees make us fall to our knees. And we should stay on our knees before God because He is worthy and trustworthy enough for us to hope in and worship Him.

Don't worry if you're not there yet: the devotions and prayers in this book will help you reach the point where you are confident that God, your heavenly Father, longs, yes longs, for you to talk to and trust Him. More than that, you will learn that God's all for you. Where you lack confidence, whether it's self-confidence or confidence in and trust in God, this book will help you know the wonderful things about God and the amazing things He does for you.

This book contains Scripture-based devotional prayers with prewritten space for you to make the prayers personal and an intimate one-on-one conversation with God. Sometimes it's difficult, when reading written prayers, to get the words to move from our heads to our hearts. Writing in your own words will make the prayers more like "heart talk"—your genuine and personal conversation with God, specific to you. I invite you to bring a journal as you work through these devotions so you can further your conversation with God. Then this book and your journal will become precious items to treasure—to look back and marvel at the intimacy of your relationship with God because you have taken the time to pray.

Each set of devotional prayers features one woman from Scripture—such as Sarah, Jochebed, and Abigail—because we can learn so much from their faith and their fears. These are women just like you and me. They face struggles and setbacks that shake their confidence and challenge their faith. But most importantly, we will learn more of the truth about God as He lovingly revealed Himself to each woman, which will strengthen our relationship and prayer life with Him.

Are you ready to begin?

A WOMAN OF HOPE
Eve

The Bible records Eve as the first female human being in the world. This position meant that Eve experienced many "firsts." Some of her experiences we cannot comprehend. She knew a perfect world and the delight of living in harmony with another human being and knowing peace with God. Other experiences of Eve's we encounter more often than we would like. She lived with broken relationships, the pain of childbirth, and the heartbreak of losing a child. She also rebelled against God's word and, as a result of that disobedience, knew a world of brokenness and pain. Eve, however, also recognized the importance of dependence on God for He is the Creator of life. Eve teaches us to cling to God because He is the one who gives us hope.

DISPLAYING GOD'S LIKENESS

Then God said, "Let us make mankind in our image, in our likeness, so that they may rule over the fish in the sea and the birds in the sky, over the livestock and all the wild animals, and over all the creatures that move along the ground." So God created mankind in his own image, in the image of God he created them; male and female he created them.

GENESIS 1:26–27

The first female human being did not, at first, have a proper name. She was not identified by a name beginning with a capital letter, personal to her. She was called "adam," which is translated "mankind."[a] Male and female human beings were *adam*. This did not mean she was insignificant. She had a clear identity. Made in the image of God, she bore the likeness of her Creator. She exhibited this likeness in common with the first male human being. Together, they bore God's likeness.

This likeness to God distinguished the first female and male humans from other living creatures. Animals were created male and female, but none had the honor of resembling their Creator. These two human beings stood out as unique in God's creation.

Being in the image of God bears huge significance. It is repeated three times in Genesis 1:26–27. However, the Bible does not specifically describe what it means to be in God's likeness. Theologians for centuries have debated

[a] "The name *Adam* (*'ā∂ām*), in addition to being a proper name, also has the connotation 'mankind,' a sense in which it occurs in the Old Testament some five hundred times, so that when the noun occurs with the definite article (*hā 'ā∂ām*), it is to be translated as the proper noun rather than as the name."[1]

^a Read Genesis 9:6 and James 3:9.

^b What is mankind that you are mindful of them, human beings that you care for them? You have made them a little lower than the angels and crowned them with glory and honor (Psalm 8:4–5).

whether likeness is in our attributes, purpose, reasoning, or the uniqueness of our relationship especially with God. Although unclear on specifics, the Bible is clear that *all* human beings bear God's likeness,^a and that it is a privilege described as being crowned "with glory and honor."^b

As a human being, you are a remarkable individual in God's world. You are distinctive. As a woman, you have dignity because God has bestowed His likeness on you. In God's eyes, your likeness to Him makes you equal to every other human being. How we see ourselves in relation to all other human beings is important, but of most importance is how we see ourselves in relation to God.

You are distinct and dignified, and you too are crowned *with glory and honor.* Pray to know your significance to God.

Lord God, You are Creator of heaven and earth, of everything in our world and beyond our world. And You have created me—in Your likeness. As I pause for a moment to think about the honor, dignity, and significance You have given me, I praise You for

_____

_____

_____.

When I think less of myself and when I tell myself I am

_____

_____,

give me a fresh understanding of the magnificence of being wonderfully made. Help me remember the worth You have bestowed upon me. Amen.

A REGAL ROLE

God blessed them and said to them, "Be fruitful and increase in number; fill the earth and subdue it. Rule over the fish in the sea and the birds in the sky and over every living creature that moves on the ground."

GENESIS 1:28

God gave the man and woman two specific instructions and responsibilities they were to perform together: to rule and increase in number.

Mankind was to be in charge of the world God had created and declared *good*. Man and woman, God's crowning creatures of creation, were to govern the world as His representatives.

To rule is a regal task. In likeness to the majestic Creator God, the man and woman were like a king and queen on earth, royal rulers over God's work. And in being royal, they had dignity.

In producing offspring, humanity would be multiplied, and people bearing God's image would populate the earth. God's people would honor God in their work. God's desire still is for the earth to be filled with His people: "For this is what the LORD says—he who created the heavens, he is God; he who fashioned and made the earth, he founded it; he did not create it to be empty, but formed it to be inhabited" (Isaiah 45:18).

The world is indeed full of people, but not everyone worships God. And humanity has ruled over the earth, but not everything we do is good.

For you and me, who worship the majestic Creator God of heaven and earth, we have a responsibility to care for God's world and for the life within it. We are to manage the world as God the Creator sees His world, as beautiful and magnificent. As God's representative, be reminded that you have been crowned with glory and honor to manage God's creation.

As we face hazardous weather conditions, the extinction of species and habitats, and environmental disasters, let's be women who do what we can with the responsibility God has given us, for the pleasure of not only our own lives but the lives of future generations.

Let's fulfill this task as an act of worship to the majestic Creator God and lead others to worship Him too as God, the Creator of life.

Let's pray about our responsibility to do what we can to take care of the world and inform others about God, the Creator of our beautiful world. Before you pray, read Psalm 104 to remind yourself of God's supervision of His creation.

Lord God, what You created You declared *good*. I'm in awe of Your creativity—and give You praise and thanks—for the exquisite beauty around me, below me, and above me.

(Read these verses from Psalm 104 (NLT), then praise and thank God in your own words.)

"You make springs pour water into the ravines, so streams gush down from the mountains. They provide water for all the animals, and the wild donkeys quench their thirst. The birds nest beside the streams and sing among the branches of the trees" (vv. 10–12).

"You made the moon to mark the seasons, and the sun knows when to set" (v. 19).

"O LORD, what a variety of things you have made! In wisdom you have made them all. The earth is full of your creatures. Here is the ocean, vast and wide, teeming with life of every kind, both large and small" (vv. 24–25).

I thank You for the splendor of

_____

_____

_____

_____

_____

A regal role

As an act of worship to You, I want to take my responsibilities seriously, and commit to looking after the breathtakingly beautiful earth You have created by (write down one way you can commit to caring for the natural world)

_____

_____

_____ .

May my act of worship lead others to know You are Creator God. Amen.

AN EZER

The LORD God said, "It is not good for the man to be alone. I will make a helper suitable for him."

GENESIS 2:18

And God said, "Let the land produce living creatures according to their kinds: the livestock, the creatures that move along the ground, and the wild animals, each according to its kind." And it was so (Genesis 1:24).

b Then God said, "Let us make mankind in our image, in our likeness, so that they may rule over the fish in the sea and the birds in the sky, over the livestock and all the wild animals, and over all the creatures that move along the ground" (Genesis 1:26).

God said, "Let the . . ." when He created the animals.[a] God said, "Let us make . . ." when He created mankind.[b] But with the creation of the first woman, God said, "I will make . . ." (Genesis 2:18). For the woman, those three words imply an intimacy in her creation.

God decided, not Adam, that man needed a suitable helper. In designing the woman to be a helper, God modeled her on a role He is known for Himself. The Hebrew word for helper is *ezer*. God is spoken about as an *ezer* in Psalm 121:1–2 where it says, "I lift up my eyes to the mountains—where does my help [*ezer*] come from? My help comes from the LORD, the Maker of heaven and earth." God is described in this psalm as one who protects and watches over His people, keeping them from harm.

Though the woman is identified as an *ezer*, God did not designate woman a lesser or subservient role. The man and woman would partner together in ruling over creation and producing offspring. They shared equal responsibility for the created world, and together they would propagate the world. In this way, the woman was the powerful counterpart to the man and completed God's creation.

As women, we have dignity and honor in our relationship with God and with others, as well as in bearing God's likeness. We have significance in our abilities and qualities. We need to remember the distinction and value God has assigned to us, and ask God to help us recover and reclaim the expansive meaning of *ezer* for ourselves.

Let's pray to know our dignity, worth, and significance.

Lord God, thank You that as a woman I am Your unique creation. Thank You that as an *ezer*, my role is modeled on one that You take on Yourself. As I think about the significance of who I am to You, I want You to be of significance to me. (Write in your own words, the relationship you want with God.)

_____

_____

_____

_____ .

Where I am misunderstood, treated disrespectfully, or _____
as a woman, remind me of the dignity with which You formed me.

As I read these devotions and spend time with You in prayer, help me to grow in my understanding of being a woman and an *ezer*. (Come back and write what you learn about living as a woman of God as you read and pray.)

_____

_____

_____

_____ .

Thank You also for the privilege of being a woman and an *ezer*. Amen.

A COMPANION

So the LORD God caused the man to fall into a deep sleep; and while he was sleeping, he took one of the man's ribs and then closed up the place with flesh. Then the LORD God made a woman from the rib he had taken out of the man, and he brought her to the man. The man said, "This is now bone of my bones and flesh of my flesh; she shall be called 'woman,' for she was taken out of man."

GENESIS 2:21–23

God created woman in a unique and distinct way. She did not come from the dust of the ground as did Adam and the animals.[a] The woman was made from a living, breathing human being.

Although unconscious throughout the procedure, Adam was conscious of the significance of God's creation when he awoke. Adam's poetic but literal exclamation "bone of my bones and flesh of my flesh" speaks to his surprise and delight.

Adam gave the first female a name—woman. The name identified her as different from himself but of the same essence. In Hebrew, the word for *woman* includes the word for *man*, just as it does in English.[b] The man and the woman were alike, but they were also different. As woman was taken from man, they had unity unlike any other creatures on earth.

Just as God decided man needed a helper, God decided, not Adam, that man needed a companion, one who was appropriately matched and satisfactorily compatible with

[a] Then the LORD God formed a man from the dust of the ground and breathed into his nostrils the breath of life, and the man became a living being (Genesis 2:7). Now the LORD God had formed out of the ground all the wild animals and all the birds in the sky (Genesis 2:19).

[b] "*Woman*—in Hebrew, 'man-ess.'"[2]

man. The forming of woman from man made them "one flesh" so they could bond and build life together. "That is why a man leaves his father and mother and is united to his wife, and they become one flesh," says Genesis 2:24.

Jesus used these words from Genesis to talk about marriage: "At the beginning the Creator 'made them male and female,' and said, 'For this reason a man will leave his father and mother and be united to his wife, and the two will become one flesh'? So they are no longer two, but one flesh. Therefore what God has joined together, let no one separate" (Matthew 19:4–6).

It can be hard to read about God's ideal and standards for marriage. We think about our own broken marriage relationships, or marriages that are far from perfect. We can be distraught that we have failed God's desire for our lives. Yet, at the same time, marriage relationships can be good. Many marriages last a lifetime. Those commitments are ones to be celebrated.

Whether you are married or unmarried, let's pray for all our relationships. Pray for yourself and those you know to experience the joy of companionship. Pray for your own marriage, or the marriages of those around you, to be strengthened with the bond of love.

Lord God, I bring before You my relationships with others. In particular, I desire to have relationships that are (write down the qualities you would like in your connections with other people)

_____

_____

_____ .

I want to know the joy of friendship as You designed it to be.

As I think about marriage, whether my own or other people's, I ask

_____

_____ .

Give me the sense to search out Your wisdom in all my relationships. Amen.

THE LURE OF MORE

When the woman saw that the fruit of the tree was good for food and pleasing to the eye, and also desirable for gaining wisdom, she took some and ate it. She also gave some to her husband, who was with her, and he ate it.

GENESIS 3:6

The honor of being God's image-bearer, the privilege of being God's representative on earth, the importance of being an *ezer*, the beauty of a special relationship with the man were not enough to satisfy the first woman.

The woman put out her hand to take what looked good rather than grasping onto the goodness of God's words: "'You must not eat fruit from the tree that is in the middle of the garden, and you must not touch it, or you will die'" (Genesis 3:3). She concluded that God was withholding something agreeable from her. *She* decided what was preferable and not what God had said was right.

God had placed a figurative boundary around the tree of the knowledge of good and evil for the good of the man and the woman. For, if they ate of it, they would die.

The woman, however, listened and decided to believe in the serpent's lies—"You will not certainly die. . . . For God knows that when you eat from it your eyes will be opened, and you will be like God, knowing good and evil" (Genesis 3:4–5)—instead of the truth of God's words and the importance of God's instruction. She wished to be more like God rather than being satisfied with bearing His likeness.

The woman with the man were meant to preside over the creatures instead of letting a creature have dominion over them.

But most of all, the woman sought "to know" independently of God.

Proverbs 1:7 (NLT) says: "Fear of the LORD is the foundation of true knowledge." God is the source of wisdom and living in relationship with

Him is our channel to understanding. We are not meant to pursue *knowing* without God, although we can and we do. We are instead to live in total dependence on Him and within the boundaries He has given us. To live wisely is to live within God's commands.

It is easy for us to want more or different than what God has prescribed for us. We can be easily dissatisfied with our lot. When temptation is in front of us, let's be women who can distinguish God's way from our own way. Let's hold onto God's words, and know they are good. Let's be women who listen to His words and obey His voice. Use this prayer based on Proverbs 3:5–6 (NLT): "Trust in the LORD with all your heart; do not depend on your own understanding. Seek his will in all you do, and he will show you which path to take."

Lord God, I want to trust in You with all my heart. (Write in your own words how you will commit to trusting God.)

_____

_____

_____ .

I promise to listen to Your words instead of trying to figure things out on my own. Forgive me for going my own way in

_____

_____ .

Help me to be able to distinguish Your will for me. Give me the wisdom to seek Your direction. (Tell God how you will commit to seeking His will on all decisions.)

_____

_____

_____ .

Amen.

27

BECOMING AWARE

Then the eyes of both of them were opened, and they realized they were naked; so they sewed fig leaves together and made coverings for themselves.

GENESIS 3:7

Rejecting God's wisdom and God's command led to new knowledge. Innocence had gone. Whereas before the man and the woman had known no shame in their nakedness, now they knew guilt and felt ashamed.

A healthy reverence for God became fear of God. So they hid. They passed blame instead of owning up. According to Adam, the woman was at fault, but God was too: "The woman you put here with me—she gave me some fruit from the tree, and I ate it" (Genesis 3:12). God had given Adam the woman. The woman blamed the serpent but at the same time told the truth: "The serpent deceived me, and I ate" (Genesis 3:13). She had indeed been deceived.

Their eyes had been opened, but they did not want to be seen by God. They no longer wanted to commune with God. Yet, God still wanted to commune with them. "Where are you?" (Genesis 3:9) God called.

It all sounds so familiar.

We do not know the beauty of living in a world without shame, guilt, and blame. We do not know a world without rebellion against God and rejection of His word. We too are deceived by so many things that often get us in trouble. We too find it hard to take the blame.

We all live with the same problem of the first couple's decision and action. We rebel against God. Ironically, when we decide to reject God, it is not that our eyes are opened to see; we become blind and senseless.

Jeremiah the prophet spoke of this devastating reality: "Hear this, you foolish and senseless people, who have eyes but do not see, who have ears but do not hear" (Jeremiah 5:21).

But we don't have to stay in that state. God can open our eyes to see the goodness of His instructions.

Jesus came to earth to open both physical and spiritual eyes that were blind. Jesus said when we look to Him, we truly see God: "For when you see me, you are seeing the one who sent me" (John 12:45 NLT).

Pray to have your eyes opened "to see the wonderful truths in your instructions" (Psalm 119:18 NLT), to know you are guilty of rebelling against God, but to also know God takes away your shame.

Lord God, I ask You to open my eyes to see where I have been rejecting Your wisdom and instructions, where I have been hiding from You. (Invite God to search your heart and mind and write down anything distancing you from Him.)

_____

_____

_____

_____

I ask for Your forgiveness, mercy, and love for the ways I have wandered from You. Thank You for taking away my shame and drawing me closer to You. Open my eyes to know the joy and wonder of following Your instructions. (Journal about the joy you find in following Him.)

_____

_____

_____

_____

_____

Amen.

FINDING HOPE

To the woman he said, "I will make your pains in childbearing very severe; with painful labor you will give birth to children. Your desire will be for your husband, and he will rule over you."

GENESIS 3:16

The woman had yet to experience childbirth, but God told her that painful contractions and difficulties in giving birth were to come. The woman had been created to complement the man and live in harmony with Adam, but now she would experience dissonance like she had not known before. Whereas both man and woman were created to rule the world together, she would live with an imbalance in their relationship.

This is the reality in which we find ourselves living. Pregnancy and childbirth are not easy and are fraught with physical risks and complications. Our relationships are filled with tension, arguments, and sometimes even abuse. And our role as a *helper* can easily be made fun of, distorted, or abused.

Yet in a difficult relationship and the pain of childbirth, hope would come through the woman and her offspring. In God's judgment on the serpent, we find this hope: "And I will put enmity between you and the woman, and between your offspring and hers; he will crush your head, and you will strike his heel" (Genesis 3:15).

In the outcome and consequences of the man and woman's rebellion, God in His graciousness did not leave them without assurance.

God does not leave us in our sin and shame without hope either. God the Creator of life brings us the promise of new life through Jesus Christ,

God's Son, "born of a woman."[a] The gospel of Luke traces the genealogy of Jesus back to Adam.[b] Jesus, born of a woman, will crush Satan's head.[c]

In the middle of the consequences of our rebellion against God, we too can find hope in God. No matter what we face today in our stressful world and difficult, draining relationships, we too can experience confidence with God through Jesus Christ.

Lord God, thank You for the hope I find in You and Your Son, Jesus. In our fallen world, I confess that many things leave me discouraged. (Share with God your disappointments and fears.)

Yet, You give many good gifts. (Write down the blessings that are life-giving and energizing to you.)

In the middle of the pain and joy I experience in life, I will remember that You are the reason for my hope. Amen.

[a] But when the right time came, God sent his Son, born of a woman, subject to the law (Galatians 4:4 NLT).

[b] Read Luke 3:23–38.

[c] The God of peace will soon crush Satan under your feet. The grace of our Lord Jesus be with you (Romans 16:20).

FINDING
OUR IDENTITY

> Adam named his wife Eve, because she would become
> the mother of all the living.
>
> GENESIS 3:20

Finally, the woman received a name. Adam called his wife *Eve*. Her name means "life."[a] Eve, however, became more than the first mother to bring a human into the world. As Genesis 3:20 explains, "She would become the mother of all the living."

Adam gave Eve her name at a significant moment. Adam realized hope would come through the woman's role as a mother just after God had announced "to dust you will return" (v. 19). Death was the result of the disregard for the commandment "You must not eat from the tree of the knowledge of good and evil, for when you eat from it you will certainly die" (2:17). In Eve, Adam saw the hope of life. Eve, given to him by God as an *ezer*, the woman he had just accused of leading him to disobey God's command, would indeed be a helper in bringing life.

Usually, we are named at birth. It is a significant moment. Our personal names have meaning and significance too. Sometimes they are part of our identity. However, it is through Jesus that we receive our fully intended identity. When we place our trust in Jesus, God gives us a new identity. We put "on the new self, which is being renewed in knowledge in the image of its Creator" (Colossians 3:10). We are renamed as children of God: "Yet to all who did receive him, to those who believed in his name, he gave the right to become children of God—children born not of natural descent, nor of human decision or a husband's will, but born of God" (John 1:12–13).

When we place our trust in Jesus, we bear His image, who is in the image of God.[a] The Bible talks about it as being clothed with Christ—"all who have been united with Christ in baptism have put on Christ, like putting on new clothes" (Galatians 3:27 NLT).

[a] The Son is the image of the invisible God, the firstborn over all creation (Colossians 1:15).

Whatever you feel you have lost in your identity—whether it is through rebellion against God, or the way you have been treated by other people—hear this: Jesus calls you "daughter." He says, "Daughter, your faith has healed you. Go in peace" (Mark 5:34).

Use this prayer to thank God for your new identity.

Lord God, I am so grateful for Jesus. I thank You for the identity that I receive through Him to be called Your child and to be called "daughter." (Take a minute to hear Jesus's words spoken to you: "Daughter, your faith has healed you. Go in peace." Tell Jesus how it feels to be called His daughter and to be seen by Him.)

Thank You, Jesus. Amen.

HELP FROM THE LORD

Adam made love to his wife Eve, and she became pregnant and gave birth to Cain. She said, "With the help of the LORD I have brought forth a man."

GENESIS 4:1

We leave Eve, the first woman and "the mother of all the living," knowing the pain of childbirth but also the joy and wonder of bringing a child into the world. Whereas Adam had marveled at the creation of the woman, Eve was almost certainly amazed at the baby who had been knit together in her womb.

We also leave Eve with the pain of losing a child. Cain killed Abel.[a] Through her disregard for the truth of God's words—"for when you eat from it you will certainly die" (Genesis 2:16–17)—Eve learned the hard way that God's words are true. Death had indeed come into the world.

Later, Eve gave birth to another son named Seth. She said: "God has granted me another child in place of Abel, since Cain killed him" (4:25). Through the birth of her children, Eve had relearned a dependence on God that she was created with and lost in her rebellion.

God did not abandon the couple when they were expelled from the garden. God was already at work to bring the hope of humanity, Jesus Christ. Seth was the child through whom God's promise of the birth of a Savior would be realized. Seth is named in the lineage of Jesus.[b]

The story of Eve began so beautifully, and although she

[a] Now Cain said to his brother Abel, "Let's go out to the field." While they were in the field, Cain attacked his brother Abel and killed him (Genesis 4:8).

[b] Read Luke 3:23–38.

rebelled against God, the story does not end there. The promise of hope has been passed down the centuries to ourselves.

Let's be women who are dependent on God for all things in our lives. Let's believe and stay true to God's Word. Let's rely on Him in the joys and the sorrows, the ups and downs, knowing that God is our help and our hope.

Make the words of Psalm 33 your prayer: "We put our hope in the LORD. He is our help and our shield. In him our hearts rejoice, for we trust in his holy name. Let your unfailing love surround us, LORD, for our hope is in you alone" (vv. 20–22 NLT).

Lord God, my heart rejoices in You, for You created me with dignity and honor, an *ezer* like Yourself. I put my trust in Your holy name (paraphrase your prayer of trust in God from day 5):

_____

_____

_____

_____ .

I place my hope in You for the days, weeks, months, and years ahead, because You are my *ezer*—my help. Be my shield and protect me from

_____

_____

_____

_____ .

Surround me with Your unfailing love. Amen.

A WOMAN ON A JOURNEY OF FAITH
Sarah

We know little about Sarah's background except that Terah was her father; Terah was also the father of her husband, Abraham. Sarah was married to her half brother.[a] Sarai began life in Ur of the Chaldeans. Biblical scholars believe Ur to be in modern-day Iraq. God spoke to Abram while he lived in Ur and told him, with Sarai, to go to the land He had promised for him.[b]

From Sarah's life we are going to learn about the life of faith and the journey of faith that we travel. We are going to see that we can have faith in the middle of impossible circumstances and major challenges. We will be encouraged by Sarah, who came from no faith to be known as a woman of faith.

[a] Besides, she really is my sister, the daughter of my father though not of my mother; and she became my wife (Genesis 20:12).

[b] The God of glory appeared to our father Abraham while he was still in Mesopotamia, before he lived in Harran. "Leave your country and your people," God said, "and go to the land I will show you."

So he left the land of the Chaldeans and settled in Harran. After the death of his father, God sent him to this land where you are now living (Acts 7:2–4).

WHEN WE ONLY SEE THE PROBLEM

Abram and Nahor both married. The name of Abram's wife was Sarai, and the name of Nahor's wife was Milkah; she was the daughter of Haran, the father of both Milkah and Iskah. Now Sarai was childless because she was not able to conceive.

GENESIS 11:29–30

In the middle of scant information about Abram and Sarai's family, the Bible gives one intimate detail: "Now Sarai was childless because she was not able to conceive." Sarai's story begins with this heartbreaking fact for her and for many other women.

Unable to conceive, Sarai would have known the cultural humiliation and shame of failing to produce an heir. In a childless marriage, women in the ancient New East were considered at fault.

In particular, male children meant a continuation of the family name. Male children inherited family land that gave economic security, especially for women. Building a family was a priority.

Being unable to conceive also meant that Sarai could not fulfill God's instruction to "be fruitful and increase in number" (Genesis 1:28).

At this time, we know nothing about Sarai's faith. We just know she faced a distressing problem that signified pressure in her marriage, vulnerability to her social standing, and looked like a lack of blessing from God.

The difficulties we encounter can affect all areas of our lives. They lead to heartbreak and being an emotional mess. They affect our relationships with other people. They can cause financial problems and insecurity in the future. Sometimes these problems creep up on us, and we have to deal with them for years. Other times we may experience catastrophe. Our emotions range from sadness to fear, deep disappointment to helplessness, and much more.

Most difficult of all is wondering where God is in all that we face. Adversity can cause us to struggle in our faith. Maybe you repeatedly asked God to come to your aid. Perhaps you are at the point where you think prayer is barely worth the effort; nothing will change. No good outcome seems possible. And if you were to be truthful, you struggle to believe God can change the situation.

Today, share your problems with God. Simply state the facts as you see them. Tell God the reality of the situation you face. Tell Him how you feel.

Lord God, these are the facts about my situation. This is the reality I face:

_____

_____

_____

_____

_____

_____.

This is how I feel:

_____

_____

_____

_____.

Thank You for listening to me. Amen.

DAY 11

GOING OUR OWN WAY

Now Sarai, Abram's wife, had borne him no children. But she had an Egyptian slave named Hagar; so she said to Abram, "The LORD has kept me from having children. Go, sleep with my slave; perhaps I can build a family through her." Abram agreed to what Sarai said.

GENESIS 16:1–2

Month after month for ten years and more, Sarai hoped to become pregnant.[a]

God had revealed His promise to Abram—"I will make you into a great nation" (Genesis 12:2)—and that Abram's offspring would be as numerous as the stars.[b]

God had made a grand promise to the couple, but Sarai's infertility stood in the way of that promise being fulfilled. And, at that point, God had not revealed how His promise would be accomplished.

God had given the instruction to be fruitful and multiply, but Sarai, as much as she wanted to, couldn't do this naturally. "The LORD has kept me from having children" (Genesis 16:2), she concluded. So Sarai came up with a solution to the problem.

Sarai followed through on what was customary in ancient times for women who faced infertility. She gave her slave to her husband to have her child.

It seemed such a simple and acceptable solution. We can sympathize with Sarai. It is hard to wait on God's answer

[a] Genesis 16:3 says Abram and Sarai "had been living in Canaan ten years." This does not include the time from the beginning of their marriage or travel from Haran.

[b] He took him outside and said, "Look up at the sky and count the stars—if indeed you can count them." Then he said to him, "So shall your offspring be" (Genesis 15:5).

41

when we can't see how a problem can be resolved. It is hard to hold onto a promise when we see only an unresolvable problem.

We too do things that seem sensible and acceptable to overcome our problems. Yet, like Sarai, we can end up making decisions independent of God instead of being fully dependent on Him.

It may be easy to say, but if Sarai thought God had stopped her from having children, she should have taken the matter to God. Sarai may have believed God would carry out His promise through their acceptable surrogacy custom, but she should have sought God's guidance on how He would fulfill His promise.

We know that God is sovereign over our lives. We know that God answers prayers. But often we think problems are ours to solve. We often seek the guidance of others before going to God. While God has given us wisdom and prudence, we often move forward with plans that seem sensible instead of waiting on God's timing and ways. Let's pray to be women who are wholly dependent on God and seek His guidance in all we do. The following prayer will help you.

Lord God, You are sovereign, and everything is under Your control. All my circumstances are safely in Your hands too. I entrust this situation to You:

———————————————————————————————————

———————————————————————————————————

——————————————————————————————————— .

I ask for Your guidance on how to respond or what to do next. (Be attentive for God's response, and journal whatever comes to mind; it's OK if you don't receive an answer immediately!)

———————————————————————————————————

———————————————————————————————————

——————————————————————————————————— .

Lord God, no matter when You respond, give me the sense to wait on Your answer and Your timing. Amen.

THE PAIN OF GOING OUR OWN WAY

Then Sarai said to Abram, "You are responsible for the wrong I am suffering. I put my slave in your arms, and now that she knows she is pregnant, she despises me. May the LORD judge between you and me." "Your slave is in your hands," Abram said. "Do with her whatever you think best." Then Sarai mistreated Hagar; so she fled from her.

GENESIS 16:5–6

Abram took Hagar as his wife, and she did indeed become pregnant. What Sarai thought was a good solution to her problem of infertility led to even more problems. Hagar began to disrespect her. She and Abram argued, and Abram didn't want anything to do with the friction in his family.

Sarai saw Abram and not herself at fault. Giving Hagar to Abram was Sarai's idea, but Sarai was so sure of her innocence that she appealed to God to be their judge.

Hagar was not innocent either. Her contempt for Sarai certainly must have added to Sarai's pain and shame. So, because Sarai could, she used her position and power to punish Hagar. Sarai did not have to retaliate or see Hagar as a rival, but she did. Sarai chose to make Hagar pay for a situation that was of her own making.

Sometimes those solutions that seemed so simple and straightforward turn out to have twists and turns and become way more complicated than we expected.

When they are, we should stop and ask ourselves, Are we too easily seeing others at fault? Are we passing the blame instead of taking responsibility for what we have created? And, like Sarai, are we lashing out at those we love? Not taking responsibility is an age-old problem. It began with Adam and Eve (day 6).

When we are responsible for making matters worse, when we have taken matters into our own hands, we should know that we can bring the messy situations we have created to God. God is the one who can give us hope in whatever circumstances we have created.

Pray about any complication you see as of your own making. Ask God for forgiveness.

Lord God, forgive me for the times I have not fully trusted in and been dependent on You. Forgive me for the times I have taken matters into my own hands and made things worse:

_____

_____

_____ .

In particular, I ask You to forgive me for (add in one or more of the following: acting out of anger, bitterness, or jealousy; being critical, quarrelsome, irritable, or . . .)_____ .

I have myself to blame. Teach me to be (write the actions and attitudes you would like to have, the opposite of what you wrote above)

_____

_____ .

Help me to make right what I have done wrong. Amen.

DISCOVERING GOD'S WAY

God also said to Abraham, "As for Sarai your wife, you are no longer to call her Sarai; her name will be Sarah. I will bless her and will surely give you a son by her. I will bless her so that she will be the mother of nations; kings of peoples will come from her."

GENESIS 17:15–16

Sarai was ninety years old when God spoke to Abraham in Genesis 17:15–16. Her womb was well past the age of holding a child.

So far, God had not been specific on how His promise to Abram would come about. However, it was clear that Ishmael, born to Abram and Sarai by Hagar, would not fulfill that promise.[a] This had been Sarai and Abram's plan, not God's plan. Instead, Sarai would give birth in her old age to a child and name him Isaac.

God's command to be fruitful and multiply, given to Adam and Eve, suddenly became God's promise: "I will make you very fruitful" (Genesis 17:6). Sarai need not have worried about her inability to fulfill God's command or feared that she had missed out on His blessing. God had a bigger blessing for Sarai.

Sarai would have a baby when it was impossible for Sarai to naturally conceive. God would choose the timing so Abram and Sarai would know it was God's accomplishment and not their own.

To mark that significant moment, God renamed Abram

[a] Abraham fell face-down; he laughed and said to himself, "Will a son be born to a man a hundred years old? Will Sarah bear a child at the age of ninety?" And Abraham said to God, "If only Ishmael might live under your blessing!" Then God said, "Yes, but your wife Sarah will bear you a son, and you will call him Isaac. I will establish my covenant with him as an everlasting covenant for his descendants after him" (Genesis 17:17–19).

and Sarai to Abraham and Sarah. Sarah means "princess." From Sarah, now a princess, would come "kings of peoples" (17:16). Sarah would become the mother of the people of Israel. Sarah is also seen as our ancestor because we are children of the promise that God made to Abraham. Our faith in Christ makes us Abraham's offspring. Romans 9:8 says: "It is not the children by physical descent who are God's children, but it is the children of the promise who are regarded as Abraham's offspring."

We may think God doesn't fulfill promises today in such astounding ways as He did for Abraham and Sarah. Yet, thousands of years later, God is still fulfilling that promise to Abraham and Sarah. It is by faith we become a child of Abraham and a child of God. The apostle Paul wrote, "Understand, then, that those who have faith are children of Abraham" (Galatians 3:7).

You and I can be amazed at what God is still doing in miraculous ways to bring about the promise given to Abraham and Sarah.

The Bible is full of other promises from God. It can be hard to hold onto God's promises when we only see unresolved problems. It can be hard to wait on God's timing. We can be confident that God keeps His promises and brings about His plans and purposes. Have faith in God's promises. Believe that God is working out His plans and purposes in the middle of your problems.

Lord God, thank You for Your promise that through faith, I am Your child. Thank You for the hope I find in Your promises. Give me the resolve to hold onto Your promises when I see only what is impossible in my life. In particular, I ask You to give me the strength to trust Your timing with

_____

_____

_____ .

(Ask God for what You need as You wait on Him in this situation.)

_____

_____

_____ .

Amen.

DAY 14

GOD OF WONDER

Now Sarah was listening at the entrance to the tent, which was behind him. Abraham and Sarah were already very old, and Sarah was past the age of childbearing. So Sarah laughed to herself as she thought, "After I am worn out and my lord is old, will I now have this pleasure?" Then the LORD said to Abraham, "Why did Sarah laugh and say, 'Will I really have a child, now that I am old?' Is anything too hard for the LORD? I will return to you at the appointed time next year, and Sarah will have a son."

GENESIS 18:10–14

God had told Abraham that Sarah would have a baby at the age of ninety. Now it seemed God intended Sarah to hear the pronouncement herself. The three men who appeared to Abraham had a message from God: "I will surely return to you about this time next year, and Sarah your wife will have a son" (Genesis 18:10). And Sarah laughed.

There was something about Sarah's laugh that prompted God to reply: "Is anything too hard for the LORD?" (Genesis 18:14). Abraham had laughed when God told him that he and Sarah would be parents at the ages of one hundred and ninety. His laugh did not prompt the same response from God. Yet in God's question to Sarah there is a wonderful truth to hold onto, perhaps one that strengthened Sarah's faith—nothing is too hard for God.[a]

God expected Sarah to believe that anything and everything was possible with God. The Hebrew word for *hard* means "wonderful" or "wondrous."[b] It is used to describe

[a] Jesus looked at them and said, "With man this is impossible, but with God all things are possible" (Matthew 19:26).

[b] "The Hebrew for 'hard' or 'difficult' (*pālā*, ' [Genesis 18:14]) means 'wonderful' (NAB) in the sense of extraordinary (e.g., Jer 32:17, 27)."[1]

47

God's work of creation: "Ah, Sovereign LORD, you have made the heavens and the earth by your great power and outstretched arm. Nothing is too hard for you," says Jeremiah 32:17.

We too can doubt God. We know everything is possible with God, but we don't see God working the same wondrous acts today as we read about in the Bible. We doubt because the problems we face seem impossible for God to change. So we pray prayers that seem possible instead of believing in God's power to do the impossible.

Yet God is wondrous, and He is wonderful. The Psalms encourage us to praise God for the wonders He has done, even in the middle of our difficulties. When we doubt God, let's instead remember the wonders He has already performed in our lives and praise Him.

Make Psalm 65:8 your prayer of praise: "The whole earth is filled with awe at your wonders; where morning dawns, where evening fades, you call forth songs of joy." Make Psalm 40:5 your prayer of thanksgiving for the wonders God has already done in your life: "Many, LORD my God, are the wonders you have done, the things you planned for us."

Lord God, I give You praise along with all of creation for

_____

_____

_____

_____

_____

_____

_____ .

Lord God, I do not want to forget the many wonders You have already done in my life. I thank You for

_____

_____

_____

_____

_____ .

And I believe You have many more wonders planned for me. Amen.

GOD THE PROMISE-KEEPER

Now the LORD was gracious to Sarah as he had said, and the LORD did for Sarah what he had promised. Sarah became pregnant and bore a son to Abraham in his old age, at the very time God had promised him.

GENESIS 21:1–2

ᵃ And the LORD visited Sarah as He had said, and the LORD did for Sarah as He had spoken (Genesis 21:1 NKJV).

God *visited* Sarah, and she became pregnant.ᵃ The magnificent and immense power and might of God came upon Sarah in its magnitude.

And Sarah exclaimed: "God has brought me laughter, and everyone who hears about this will laugh with me" (Genesis 21:6). Sarah had laughed to herself in disbelief at God's promise. Now she laughed out loud with joy and delight at God's goodness. She laughed with elation at God's miracle, of doing the impossible. Now, she knew nothing was too hard for God.

God fulfilled His promise in His timing so Sarah and all those who know her story would know the greatness of God. God's promise remained certain even in the middle of Sarah's doubt.

God is a promise-keeper. Psalm 145:13 (NLT) reminds us: "The LORD always keeps his promises; he is gracious in all he does." God's promises, spoken to you through the Bible, remain certain too. Hold on tight to God's promises.

God promises to: hear your cries (Psalm 10:17), show compassion (Psalm 116:5–6), comfort you (2 Corinthians 1:3–4), never forsake you (Psalm 9:10), guide you (Psalm

32:8), provide for you (Philippians 4:19), restore joy (Psalm 126:5–6), give you protection (Psalm 34:7).

Choose one of God's promises listed above, or find your own, and pray for God to be gracious to you. Ask Him to visit you in His might and power regarding the situation you prayed about on the first day of this section on Sarah, day 10, so you will be able to laugh with delight at God's goodness.

Lord God, Your promises are sure and true. I ask You to be gracious to me; visit me with Your might and power. In my current situation, I ask You to

_____

_____ .

Hear my cries and desires, for You are the God who listens (Psalm 10:17). Listen and encourage me by

_____

_____ .

Protect me, for You are full of compassion (Psalm 116:5–6). Save me from

_____

_____ .

Comfort me in my troubles, for You are the God of all comfort (2 Corinthians 1:3–4). Bring me contentment by

_____ .

Never forsake me, for You are a God who can be trusted (Psalm 9:10). Do not leave me to

_____

_____ .

Guide me, for You are the God who instructs (Psalm 32:8). Reveal the step I should take in

_____

_____ .

Equip me, for You are the God who provides for all my needs (Philippians 4:19). Meet my need of

_____

_____ .

Sustain me, for You are my shield (Psalm 34:7). Lift my head high so I can

_____

_____ .

Amen.

LETTING GO

The child grew and was weaned, and on the day Isaac was weaned Abraham held a great feast. But Sarah saw that the son whom Hagar the Egyptian had borne to Abraham was mocking, and she said to Abraham, "Get rid of that slave woman and her son, for that woman's son will never share in the inheritance with my son Isaac."

GENESIS 21:8–10

In our last devotion, Sarah laughed with delight because God had been gracious to her. Sarah had seen and experienced that God had kept His promise. Sarah's shame had gone. She'd given her husband an heir. She had a future as the mother of kings.

Yet Sarah's laughter was curtailed by Ishmael's mocking laughter of Isaac.

The old animosity between Sarah and Hagar still existed. Sarah had not taken Ishmael as her son, which had been the intention of giving her slave to her husband. Instead, Ishmael was "that woman's son" (Genesis 21:10). Sarah never once called Hagar by her name. Her loathing of Hagar is heard in the finality of her statement, Ishmael would *never* share in Isaac's inheritance. God had been gracious to Sarah, but Sarah could not bring herself to be gracious to Hagar.

We have just prayed for God to shower us with His graciousness in our lives and for God to visit us with His might and power in our problems. Yet, at the same time, there can be areas in our lives where we are not being gracious to other people. Maybe you are still blaming someone else or making a person pay for the messy situation created by taking matters into your own hands. Maybe your wounds are still too fresh for you to be kind to them.

We want God to graciously make possible the impossible in our lives. Let's be women who, as hard or impossible as it might be, extend God's graciousness to other people, particularly those who have hurt us, those we are in conflict with, and those we dislike.

Pray to be kind or merciful, or let go of an old animosity.

Lord God, as I make steps forward in trusting You, being dependent on Your goodness and graciousness, I am becoming a woman of faith. Yet there are areas in my life where I am not gracious to others. I ask Your forgiveness for my words and behaviors:

_____

_____

_____ .

(Below, take the words of Colossians 4:5–6 and apply them to your situation.) Just as You are gracious to me, give me the strength to . . .

"Be wise in the way you act toward outsiders."

_____

_____ .

"Make the most of every opportunity."

_____

_____ .

"Let your conversation be always full of grace, seasoned with salt, so that you may know how to answer everyone."

_____

_____

_____

_____ .

Amen.

BEING A WOMAN OF FAITH

And by faith even Sarah, who was past childbearing age, was enabled to bear children because she considered him faithful who had made the promise.

HEBREWS 11:11

Sarah is remembered for her faith. She is celebrated for believing that God would keep His promise.

The last we read about Sarah, she banished Hagar and Ishmael from her home. But Sarah is not remembered for her poor behavior. We know nothing more about Sarah except that she died at the age of 127 and Abraham mourned losing her (Genesis 23:1–2). Yet most of all Sarah was commended for her faith.

Sarah is ultimately respected for trusting God with her barrenness, not for holding Him responsible for it. Sarah is, most importantly, recognized for waiting for God to carry out His promise, not for acting on her own to bring about His promise. Sarah is, in the end, praised for her belief that God would revive her dead womb, not for laughing with doubt because the possibility of having a baby was too late.

The journey of faith we have been on with Sarah has not been easy. But that is so true for our journeys of faith too. Sarah knew deep disappointment and enormous heartache in her life, along with the pain of suffering the disdain of others. Yet Sarah gives us confidence that even though our lives are messy and hard, and our faith is at times faulty and weak, God still keeps His promises to us.

Sarah encourages us to trust in God and believe He is able to overcome all things. We focus our attention on God's might and power, who can bring new life out of a dead womb, whose timing is perfect, and whose plans and purposes are always good.

You may not like God's timing. You may want to help or hurry God along, but "let us hold tightly without wavering to the hope we affirm, for God can be trusted to keep his promise" (Hebrews 10:23 NLT).

Let's be women of faith, who believe God is faithful to His promises. When life seems impossible, when the unfulfilled promises stretch out before us, we need to remember that God always keeps to His promises and He is faithful. Say this prayer.

Heavenly Father, even though my faith is faulty and far from perfect, I am thankful that my hope is not based on who I am but on who You are. I began this journey of faith seeing only the impossible before me. (Summarize what you wrote in your prayer at the beginning of this journey with Sarah, on day 10, about an area of your life where you need fresh hope and faith.)

_____

_____

_____ .

Today, I see that You are perfectly faithful in all that You do for me. You are the God of wonders who has already done wonderful things in my life. (Write in what you thanked God for on day 14):

_____

_____

_____ .

You are a promise-keeper. (Write down one promise from your prayer on day 15 that spoke to you.)

_____ .

When I see only problems ahead of me, I will remember Your faithfulness. I place my trust in You, Your plans and purposes, and Your perfect timing. Amen.

A WOMAN WHO EXPERIENCED GOD'S PRESENCE
Hagar

Hagar was the slave of Sarai. Hagar didn't just work for Sarai; she was her personal property. We do not know how Hagar came to be owned by Sarai, but it is possible Sarai acquired Hagar while she and Abram lived in Egypt.[a] However, we do know Hagar lived with Abram and Sarai far away from her Egyptian homeland. We also know Hagar was young and fertile enough to have children, whereas Sarai was not.

Being owned by another person can be hard to understand when we have so many freedoms. But slavery deprived Hagar of most, if not all, rights we are used to. Hagar had to do everything Sarai asked of her. She had no freedom of her own. Except, we will discover, Hagar had freedom over her thoughts and her attitude.

Today, the concept of slavery is abhorrent. However, during ancient biblical times, slavery was a widely accepted practice. Men, women, and children became slaves for a

[a] Now there was a famine in the land, and Abram went down to Egypt to live there for a while because the famine was severe (Genesis 12:10).

variety of reasons with varied experiences. We may not be able to fully relate to Hagar's life as a slave, but we can learn much from her life how God sees, hears, and cares about every situation in our lives.

OWNING OUR ATTITUDE

So after Abram had been living in Canaan ten years, Sarai his wife took her Egyptian slave Hagar and gave her to her husband to be his wife. He slept with Hagar, and she conceived. When she knew she was pregnant, she began to despise her mistress.

GENESIS 16:3–4

Hagar had no choice in becoming Abram's wife. *Wife* did not elevate Hagar to the same status as Sarai. Instead, Hagar had to comply with a form of surrogacy, customary during Old Testament times, that enabled barren wives to have children. Hagar's baby would become Abram and Sarai's child.

Hagar also had no choice over how Sarai used her, but she did have a choice over how she reacted. Hagar chose to ridicule—"to despise"—Sarai (Genesis 16:4).

To *despise* someone means to "make small" and to make the other "feel insignificant." The Hebrew word can also mean to "declare cursed." To be cursed is the opposite of blessing. *Cursed* implied Sarai had not been blessed by God in being fruitful with children.

It's not difficult to think Hagar had justifiable reasons for her attitude toward Sarai. Perhaps to Hagar, her fertility in contrast to Sarai's infertility transformed her from inferior to superior, worthless to worthwhile, and powerless to powerful.

Today, someone having power over our bodies is never acceptable. We are justified in putting it right. Where we have smaller liberties taken away or have been taken advantage of in minor ways, however, we too can feel warranted in having a bad attitude, and even excuse ourselves for being that way.

No matter what, we have infinite worth, but we may feel unappreciated, insignificant, or unacknowledged at home or work. A roll of the eyes, a scoff, seems an acceptable response. Being sarcastic or making unkind comments to knock the other person's confidence can be satisfying.

The Bible, however, invites us to have a different response. To treat others well, even those who treat us badly: "Bless those who persecute you; bless and do not curse" (Romans 12:14).

We are challenged not to think more highly of ourselves than of others. The apostle Paul wrote, "Do nothing out of selfish ambition or vain conceit. Rather, in humility value others above yourselves, not looking to your own interests but each of you to the interests of the others" (Philippians 2:3–4).

Our posture toward others and our responses whatever their attitude need to be God-honoring. Take a moment to think about those you have treated badly. Use this prayer to ask God for forgiveness.

Lord God, You've seen when I put someone down or make them feel small by (write in the behaviors or words you have used)

You know the satisfaction it's given me to do so because I feel

---

Even though what may have been done to me is inexcusable, this does not excuse my response. I confess I am wrong. I ask You to forgive me. In future situations, I ask You to give me the wisdom and ability to "bless those who persecute you; bless and do not curse" (Romans 12:14), and to "value others above yourselves, not looking to your own interests but each of you to the interests of the others" (Philippians 2:3–4). Amen.

SHOWING HUMILITY

"Your slave is in your hands," Abram said. "Do with her whatever you think best." Then Sarai mistreated Hagar; so she fled from her.

GENESIS 16:6

Sarai reacted and retaliated to Hagar's haughty attitude. The word *mistreated* means "to oppress and humiliate, to do violence." It can also mean to "crouch" or "hunch up," which gives a visual picture of Hagar's suffering.

As Sarai's slave, Hagar would have been powerless to stop Sarai's mistreatment. Hagar had no control over how she was treated. Abram also took no responsibility, even though Hagar carried his child. Instead, Abram gave Sarai full authority over Hagar. The only way Hagar could get out of the abusive situation was to run away.

There was no excuse for Sarai's behavior. Likewise, there is no excuse for those who abuse us. If you are in a situation where you are made to feel powerless, or if you are being abused, it is important to seek help.

However, when we've made a comment, even if unintentional, and we've hurt or humiliated someone, it's not unusual to have pain inflicted back. Retaliation is a common response. We may, like Hagar, be desperate to avoid or ignore what is going on.

We cannot control the reactions of other people when we have hurt them. But we do have control over the way we respond. They may not forgive us even when we apologize. But, as we've already discovered, we have an opportunity to change our own behavior. What reaction are you facing from hurting someone? Where do you need to back down and even apologize? Let's pray to be women who conduct ourselves well and use our words wisely.

Lord God, help me to realize when my behavior or words, intentional or unintentional, have caused pain and humiliation. Give me the insight to recognize reactions from others that are retaliation. (Tell God about some reactions you have received.)

_____

_____

_____ .

When my natural reaction is to not back down, to ignore what has happened and avoid dealing with the situation, and even to not apologize when I know I should, show me how to respond. (Read Colossians 3:12–14 [NLT] below. Then respond as God prompts you.)

"Since God chose you to be the holy people he loves, you must clothe yourselves with tenderhearted mercy, kindness, humility, gentleness, and patience. Make allowance for each other's faults, and forgive anyone who offends you. Remember, the Lord forgave you, so you must forgive others. Above all, clothe yourselves with love, which binds us all together in perfect harmony."

Lord, I believe You are asking me to

_____

_____

_____ .

Thank You for giving me the wisdom and humility to conduct myself well and use my words wisely. Amen.

GOD'S WAY

The angel of the LORD found Hagar near a spring in the desert; it was the spring that is beside the road to Shur. And he said, "Hagar, slave of Sarai, where have you come from, and where are you going?" "I'm running away from my mistress Sarai," she answered. Then the angel of the LORD told her, "Go back to your mistress and submit to her."

GENESIS 16:7–9

Hagar had lost the strength to continue on in a home where she was mistreated. She resorted to the desperate action of running away. In doing so, she had no protection, food, water, or future. Being pregnant and alone in the desert left her vulnerable with little chance of survival.

God, however, cared about Hagar. She may only have been a slave, with an inferior status in Abram's family, but Hagar was of significance to God. God sent "the angel of the LORD,"[a] His personal messenger, to find Hagar, to stop her and give her guidance (Genesis 16:7).

Running away was not part of God's plan for Hagar. The angel gave Hagar instructions to return to the security of Abram's household.

We should not interpret the angel's instruction to mean we should stay in violent and abusive relationships. Professionals exist to help provide protection and a safe place to stay.

Sometimes what God wants us to do is not easy. Sometimes, when we are bickering, it might mean facing up to a situation we don't like. Other times we can feel so

[a] Many scholars believe that the angel of the Lord was the preincarnate Christ.

miserable we have a hard time seeing any good in where we are and what we are doing. Often, when we are arguing over petty and trivial matters, we need to consider apologizing even if we don't want to.

In Psalm 32:8 (NLT) God says: "I will guide you along the best pathway for your life. I will advise you and watch over you."

Use this prayer—which is written as if God is speaking directly to you—to seek God's guidance for the situations you face.

(Write your name.) _____ ,
I am the God who sees your pain and misery. Sometimes, doing the right thing is not easy. Remember what you wrote in your prayer yesterday? (Write down again how God prompted you to respond.)

_____

_____

_____ .

I am always present, close at hand, ready to lead you. Listen for My voice and direction in these words: "The LORD will guide you continually, giving you water when you are dry and restoring your strength. You will be like a well-watered garden, like an ever-flowing spring" (Isaiah 58:11 NLT).

(Tell God where, when, and with whom you want Him to guide you.) Lord God, I ask You to guide me

_____

_____

_____

_____ .

Amen.

STAYING POWER

The angel added, "I will increase your descendants so much that they will be too numerous to count."

The angel of the LORD also said to her: "You are now pregnant and you will give birth to a son. You shall name him Ishmael, for the LORD has heard of your misery."

GENESIS 16:10–11

The angel of the Lord didn't just give Hagar a command to follow. He gave her a promise to hold onto. Hagar, a powerless enslaved woman, is the first woman in the Bible to receive a personal promise from God. That promise echoed the promise given to Abram, for Hagar carried his son. "'Look up at the sky and count the stars—if indeed you can count them.' Then he said to him, 'So shall your offspring be'" (Genesis 15:5). God gave Hagar hope in the middle of her suffering.

Hagar needed enormous courage and resolve to return to a home of animosity. Yet God's words of promise and assurance gave Hagar the motivation she needed. Ishmael's name would remind her that *God hears* her cries in her misery.[a]

Yesterday you learned that God is present and ready to guide you. To follow God's way takes courage. Courage, though, does not take place in the absence of pain and problems but in the middle of them. And often, God's instruction means having courage to stay put in our problems and not try to escape them. Yet we are not courageous alone. Hagar's story assures us that no matter how powerless or worthless we feel, God sees and God hears. God cares for

a "*Ishmael* means 'El [God] hears' (*yišmāʿēʾ1*), commemorating the Lord who 'heard' (*šāmaʿ*) her 'affliction' (*ʿonî*, 'misery,' NIV [Genesis 16:11])."[1]

65

you. God does not expect you to have courage to stay put in the absence of assurances but in the strength of His promises that He is with you.

Make these promises your prayer.

Lord God, give me the strength and the courage to have staying power in the middle of my pain and problems. I will hold onto Your promises. (Read the Bible verses below, then write your own words of praise and thanksgiving to God alongside each promise.)

"Where can I go from your Spirit? Where can I flee from your presence? If I go up to the heavens, you are there; if I make my bed in the depths, you are there. If I rise on the wings of the dawn, if I settle on the far side of the sea, even there your hand will guide me" (Psalm 139:7–10). I praise You for

_____

_____

_____ .

"The LORD is near to all who call on him, to all who call on him in truth" (Psalm 145:18). I thank You for

_____ .

"The LORD is close to the brokenhearted and saves those who are crushed in spirit" (Psalm 34:18). I thank You for

_____ .

"Even though I walk through the darkest valley, I will fear no evil, for you are with me; your rod and your staff, they comfort me" (Psalm 23:4). I praise You for

_____

_____ .

Amen.

"THE GOD WHO SEES ME"

She gave this name to the LORD who spoke to her: "You are the God who sees me," for she said, "I have now seen the One who sees me." That is why the well was called Beer Lahai Roi; it is still there, between Kadesh and Bered.

GENESIS 16:13–14

Through her conversation with the angel of the Lord, Hagar came to a personal understanding of God's protection. Hagar gave God a new name, one He had not been known by—*El Roi*, The God Who Sees Me. This insignificant woman felt seen by the almighty God in her misery and wretchedness. But God didn't just see. He didn't just watch what was happening with Hagar, God took action, and He intervened. God found her. He searched her out. God came to Hagar with a wondrous promise, full of hope. Hagar would have descendants too numerous to count.

Through God's promise, Hagar drew strength to obey God's instruction and to continue on. In her moment of despair, Hagar experienced God's presence. She was not alone in her desperation. God promised to protect Hagar and give her a future.

In your moments of despair, God is with you too. God hears your cries. God sees your suffering. You may be in a situation where all hope has gone and there are no choices left for you, or so it seems. Like Hagar, you can pour out praise to God, and place your trust and hope in Him because not only does God see you, but you "see" Him. How have you been reassured of God's presence so far, come to a fresh understanding about God, or experienced His provision? Use your own words to describe His goodness.

El Roi, the God who sees me, I now see You with new eyes and a fresh understanding. Here is what I have learned about You:

_____

_____

_____

_____ .

As I come to a greater understanding of Your protection, this is the personal name I want to give to You. (Write from your heart. Don't worry if your words aren't eloquent.)

_____

_____

_____ .

Amen.

NEVER ALONE

So Hagar bore Abram a son, and Abram gave the name Ishmael to the son she had borne. . . . On the day Isaac was weaned Abraham held a great feast. But Sarah saw that the son whom Hagar the Egyptian had borne to Abraham was mocking, and she said to Abraham, "Get rid of that slave woman and her son, for that woman's son will never share in the inheritance with my son Isaac."

GENESIS 16:15; 21:8–10

Hagar went back to Sarai and Abram's household and gave birth to a boy, just as the angel of the Lord had told her. Abram named the boy Ishmael, just as God had instructed Hagar.

Years later, when Ishmael was a teenager, Ishmael mocked Isaac, Sarah's son, reminding us of Hagar's attitude toward Sarai. We can wonder if Ishmael learned his mocking from his mother. This time Sarah didn't mistreat Hagar, causing her to run away; she demanded that Hagar and Ishmael leave the household for good. Whereas before God sent Hagar back, this time God told Abraham to follow through on Sarah's request. Once again, Hagar found herself in a desperate situation in the desert, with not only her own life in danger but that of her child too.

Abraham attempted to provide for his wife and child: "Early the next morning Abraham took some food and a skin of water and gave them to Hagar. He set them on her shoulders and then sent her off with the boy" (Genesis 21:14). A skin of water does not last long in the hot desert.

Hagar "wandered in the Desert of Beersheba" (21:14). She didn't know what to do or in which direction to go. Whereas last time in the desert she had found a spring, this time she had no source of fresh water. So "she put the boy under one of the bushes. Then she went off and sat down about a bowshot away, for she thought, 'I cannot watch the boy die.' And as she sat there, she began to sob" (vv. 15–16).

We feel for Hagar in her despair and helplessness. We wonder why God let this happen. God who saw her, heard her, and made a promise to her seemed to have turned His back on her.

Sometimes God allows things to happen in our lives that seem harsh. We've put our trust in Him and His promises, but things do not go right. A sudden life-threatening diagnosis, an unexpected job loss, a relationship ending, a death. Even the situation you have been praying about so far may have gone from bad to worse. During occasions like this, we can hit rock bottom. We can feel lost, aimless, and we wonder where God is and why He has allowed it to happen. Sometimes we can't even pray.

The Bible reminds us what God promises: "I will never leave you nor forsake you" (Joshua 1:5). Bring your fear and discouragement to God.

Lord God, I could sit down and sob. I've put my faith and trust in You, but still things in life do not go right. I am afraid

_____

_____

_____ .

I am discouraged because

_____

_____ .

I confess that I question why You allow difficult situations to happen. Reassure me that I am never alone, that You are always with me. Let me feel Your presence today. Remind me that You see me and You hear me so I can praise You again. (When you receive that reassurance, describe your experience and give thanks to God.)

_____

_____ .

Amen.

ACTIVE OBEDIENCE

God heard the boy crying, and the angel of God called to Hagar from heaven and said to her, "What is the matter, Hagar? Do not be afraid; God has heard the boy crying as he lies there. Lift the boy up and take him by the hand, for I will make him into a great nation."

GENESIS 21:17–18

"What is the matter, Hagar?" (Genesis 21:17). It seems like such a silly question. God saw everything that went on with Hagar. God knew what was wrong. Why bother to ask the question?

The question conveys compassion and concern. But there is more. The question is followed up with reason for hope and confirmation that God's promise to Hagar still stood.

Hagar feared for the life of her child and for her future. Without a son, Hagar had no one to provide for her. The angel of the Lord didn't wait for her to answer His question. Instead, He instructed her: "Do not be afraid" (v. 17). God eased her fears by confirming Ishmael would not only live but he would also be the father of a great nation.

It seems Hagar had forgotten the promise God had given her the last time she was in the desert: "I will increase your descendants so much that they will be too numerous to count" (Genesis 16:10).

God would provide for Hagar and her son. However, Hagar had to show active obedience. She had to "lift the boy up and take him by the hand" (21:18).

When we're in the middle of a desperate and frightening situation, we too tend to forget that God has promised to never leave us. We too forget that God's Word says over and over again to not be afraid. Perhaps you are concerned about your future security, have no one to care for you in old age, or have insufficient finances. Maybe you feel like you are wandering in a desert with nowhere to go, and no one to support you.

Often we have to step out in active obedience too, even if it means getting out of bed in the morning believing that God will come through for us.

God, sometimes I can't see beyond my fears and the difficult situation I am in. But I will not forget the promises You have made to me. I am reminded that (choose one of the promises from the prayer on day 21 and write it in your own words here)

_____

_____

_____ .

I will trust in Your promise to me and step out in faith instead of shrinking back in fear. I will (write down one act of obedience you can take to show your faith in God)

_____

_____

_____

_____ .

Amen.

EYES TO SEE

Then God opened her eyes and she saw a well of water. So she went and filled the skin with water and gave the boy a drink. God was with the boy as he grew up. He lived in the desert and became an archer. While he was living in the Desert of Paran, his mother got a wife for him from Egypt.

GENESIS 21:19–21

El Roi, The God Who Sees Me, now gave Hagar eyes to see His provision. We assume Hagar followed God's instructions and went to Ishmael, and *then* she saw the well of water. Abraham had given Hagar a limited amount of drinking water when he sent her away. That provision had been consumed. In her fear, Hagar could not see beyond the plight that she and her son were in. God met Hagar's physical needs by opening her eyes to see what was right in front of her—a well of water. God provided a lasting supply of water from a well.

God had seen Hagar and Ishmael's misery. Then Hagar saw God's abundant provision.

Fear can blind us to God's promises that He sees us, He hears us, and He protects us. Fear causes us to focus on what we don't have instead of what God can provide. Fear can stop us from stepping out in faith.

Our nearsightedness can stop us from seeing God's long-lasting goodness, even though it is right in front of us. God's promises in the Bible are endless; they last for eternity. He promises to strengthen us, to go before us, to give us perfect peace, to make our steps firm, to lighten our burdens . . .

Ask God to give you eyes to see His provision. His provision might be immediate or His provision may be in the future, and you have to wait in faith. Yet the God in whom you trust is generous. He will provide beyond your expectations and "is able to do immeasurably more than all we ask or imagine" (Ephesians 3:20). God promises to meet *"all"* your needs from his glorious riches, which have been given to us in Christ Jesus" (Philippians 4:19 NLT, emphasis added). God is generous in giving good gifts to His children who ask Him.

Jesus reassures us, "If you, then, though you are evil, know how to give good gifts to your children, how much more will your Father in heaven give good gifts to those who ask him!" (Matthew 7:11).

Be ready to be surprised by God's abundant provision.

Lord God, You are the One who sees me. I praise You because You are present with me, You give me promises to hold on to, and You provide for me. Yesterday, I put my trust in You and stepped out in faith by (write down the act of obedience you have taken)

_____

_____

_____ .

Now, Lord God, open my eyes. Give me eyes to see Your abundant provision that is right in front of me—one that I don't want to miss. (As you notice the ways in which God is providing for you, write them down here so you can come back and be reminded that He sees you, hears you, and cares for you.)

_____

_____

_____ .

Thank you, Lord God, for meeting all my needs. Amen.

AN OVERENTHUSIASTIC WOMAN
Rebekah

Abraham and Sarah were Rebekah's great-uncle and great-aunt.[a] Abraham's brother Nahor and his wife, Milkah, had eight sons. Rebekah was the child of Bethuel, the youngest son. We are to remember at that time, it was customary for marriages to take place within families.

Abraham was very old and instructed his servant to find a wife for his son Isaac from among his relatives and not from among the Canaanites with whom he was living. We begin the story of Rebekah with Abraham's servant having arrived in the land where Abraham's family lived.

In Rebekah's story, we discover that prayer plays an important part in God bringing about His purposes, but at the same time actions, good or bad, do not obstruct God's purposes.

[a] Bethuel became the father of Rebekah. Milkah bore these eight sons to Abraham's brother Nahor (Genesis 22:23).

LIVING EXPECTANTLY

Before he had finished praying, Rebekah came out with her jar on her shoulder. She was the daughter of Bethuel son of Milkah, who was the wife of Abraham's brother Nahor. The woman was very beautiful, a virgin; no man had ever slept with her. She went down to the spring, filled her jar and came up again. The servant hurried to meet her and said, "Please give me a little water from your jar."

GENESIS 24:15–17

Although Rebekah didn't know it, as she walked toward the spring that day, she was an answer to prayer. As she carried out the same mundane task she did every day, this day would be completely different. Abraham's hopes for his son would be satisfied. The servant's mission would be successful, and God's promise to Abraham would continue to be fulfilled. God was at work.

Abraham instructed his servant to find a wife for Isaac from his relatives: "Swear by the LORD, the God of heaven and the God of earth, that you will not get a wife for my son from the daughters of the Canaanites, among whom I am living, but will go to my country and my own relatives and get a wife for my son Isaac" (Genesis 24:3–4).

Abraham reassured his servant that God would guide him: "The LORD, the God of heaven, who brought me out of my father's household and my native land and who spoke to me and promised me on oath, saying, 'To your offspring I will give this land'—he will send his angel before you so that you can get a wife for my son from there" (Genesis 24:7).

The servant sensibly decided the best way of possibly meeting a relative of Abraham's and a possible wife would be at a place where "daughters of the townspeople are coming out to draw water" (Genesis 24:13). At the same time, he prayed confidently and specifically: "May it be that when I say to a young woman, 'Please let down your jar that I may have a drink,' and she says, 'Drink, and I'll water your camels too'—let her be the one you have chosen for your servant Isaac" (v. 14). And so Rebekah and the servant met.

"Before he had finished praying" (v. 15), Rebekah appeared on the scene.

Rebekah's story begins by suggesting for our consideration that God is in control of putting the right people in the right place at the right time to bring about His purposes. We also learn that God allows our prayers to play a part in His plans.

We love to see God at work in this way. We call these moments "divine appointments." We feel encouraged when we're an answer to someone's prayer. It's heartening to know we can be used in God's plans.

Even in the middle of our day-to-day, ordinary tasks, God can use us. Let's be women who live each day expectantly, making ourselves available to God.

Whatever you do today, ask God to make it extraordinary for yourself and the people you meet. Perhaps you will satisfy someone's hopes, enable God's purposes to be fulfilled, and be an answer to someone's prayer.

Lord God, thank You for the ways You bring about Your good purposes and plans in my life. (Thank God for an instance in which you saw Him work in and through the ordinary.)

_____

_____

_____ .

As I go about my regular day-to-day tasks of (make a list of what you do each day, especially those things that can seem mundane)

_____

_____ ,

I will wait expectantly for divine appointments. I want to be available for Your purposes today. May I satisfy someone's hopes, be an answer to prayer, and enable the ordinary to be extraordinary. Amen.

LIVING ENTHUSIASTICALLY

"Drink, my lord," she said, and quickly lowered the jar to her hands and gave him a drink. After she had given him a drink, she said, "I'll draw water for your camels too, until they have had enough to drink." So she quickly emptied her jar into the trough, ran back to the well to draw more water, and drew enough for all his camels. Without saying a word, the man watched her closely to learn whether or not the Lord had made his journey successful.

GENESIS 24:18–21

Rebekah's generosity and accommodating attitude seem so natural. She worked quickly and enthusiastically, running to the well, water splashing as she filled the troughs. In doing so, Rebekah answered the servant's prayer. When she learned that the servant had come from her relatives in a distant land, she ran excitedly back to her family (Genesis 24:26–27). We can imagine her bursting in upon her family, bubbling with excitement as she retold the story of her encounter at the well.

Rebekah comes across as refreshingly bighearted and pleasantly exuberant. In doing so, she was blissfully unaware that God was using her natural qualities to answer the man's prayer. Rebekah had contributed, by her behavior, in making the servant's journey a success.

Rebekah's attitude encourages us to live in the same way. We *should* live the life God has given us with enthusiasm. We *should* live each day being as generous as we can be. We *should* excitedly hope for divine appointments each day. For some of us this comes more naturally than for others. To encourage those of us who find it harder to be outgoing, Proverbs 11:25 may help us to do our best. For in being generous, "whoever refreshes others will be refreshed."

Pray to live each day with enthusiasm for God. Ask God to give you opportunities to be bighearted, not just to those you know and love, but to strangers and outsiders.

Lord God, may I live each day with energy, excitement, and enthusiasm for the good things You have planned for me. Today, as I (fill in with activities you will be doing today)

_____

_____

_____ ,

give me opportunities to be generous, hospitable, and hardworking.

Even now, would You bring to mind any ways that I can be generous to or mindful of others today. (Be attentive for God's response and write down whatever comes to mind here.)

_____

_____

_____

_____ .

As I refresh others, I look forward to being refreshed by You. Amen.

DAY 28

GOD'S PROVIDENCE

Laban and Bethuel answered, "This is from the LORD; we can say nothing to you one way or the other. Here is Rebekah; take her and go, and let her become the wife of your master's son, as the LORD has directed."

GENESIS 24:50–51

The encounter at the well, the answer to the servant's prayer, and the telling of Abraham's story meant that Rebekah's family were assured that "this is from the LORD" (Genesis 24:50). God had led the servant to the well to where Rebekah came to draw water.

God had guided and led Abraham's servant that day to the well.[a] Just like Abraham said God would: "He will send his angel before you so that you can get a wife for my son from there" (24:7).

God directed everything for the purpose of fulfilling the next step in His promise to make Abraham's descendants as numerous as the stars.

God providing and guiding for His purposes is called God's providence. *God's providence* is linked closely to God's sovereign reign over everything on earth and in the heavens. God has absolute authority and power to do as He pleases. This includes God providing for our good and guiding for His purposes.

God was in the details that day, governing the movements of Rebekah and the servant for His very desires.

Knowing that God leads and directs our circumstances can encourage us to have a confident trust in God like

[a] And I bowed down and worshiped the LORD. I praised the LORD, the God of my master Abraham, who had led me on the right road to get the granddaughter of my master's brother for his son (Genesis 24:48).

81

Abraham, for "he will send his angel before you" (24:7). Knowing that God leads and directs our circumstances can teach us to pray confidently and specifically like Abraham's servant. Knowing that God does everything according to His purposes can empower us to go about our day eagerly and expectantly like Rebekah.

Let's take note of where God has been guiding and providing in our lives so we can confidently trust God with every circumstance we encounter. Give praise to God for an event where you have known "This is from the LORD" (v. 50).

Lord God, I praise You for guiding and providing for me when

_____

_____

_____

_____

_____ .

Amen.

BEING WILLING

When they got up the next morning, he said, "Send me on my way to my master." But her brother and her mother replied, "Let the young woman remain with us ten days or so; then you may go." But he said to them, "Do not detain me, now that the LORD has granted success to my journey. Send me on my way so I may go to my master." Then they said, "Let's call the young woman and ask her about it." So they called Rebekah and asked her, "Will you go with this man?" "I will go," she said.

GENESIS 24:54–58

His prayer successfully answered and his mission complete, Abraham's servant wanted to return immediately to Canaan with Rebekah.

Rebekah's family, on the other hand, wanted to delay the departure. It seems like a normal request for a family of any era. A long journey and an upcoming marriage needed preparation. From living under the same roof to not seeing each other is enough to make one linger before having to say goodbye to a loved one.

Again we observe the same eagerness and exuberance from Rebekah as we've seen before. Perhaps somewhat surprisingly, Rebekah responded with an open and generous "I will go" (Genesis 24:58). Rebekah did not delay in following God's plans for her. Sometimes God's purposes have to be considered as more important than what is customary or desired.

So far we have prayed to be an answer to someone else's prayer. We've prayed for opportunities to be bighearted. We've praised God for guiding and providing for our lives. Now we come to a crunch point. If God has or does ask us to go, wherever that might be or whatever it might be, would we be willing?

Sometimes saying "I will go" to God's purposes is easy. There is not too much required of us. Other times it involves a major decision and a difficult choice. Even though life up to now has been ordinary, suddenly we are faced with a huge and extraordinary call. God may ask you to leave behind people you love, a job you enjoy, or the place you call home. Maybe, like Rebekah, you have family, friends, or colleagues wanting to hold you back.

When that time comes, and you lack the courage to respond with enthusiasm, remember that God goes with you. You can trust that if He's calling you, God will go before you and empower you to do what you cannot do on your own.

Let's pray to be women who are eager and willing to go whenever and wherever we see God at work, to be willing to join Him there.

Use the prayer below to help you.

Lord God, whenever and wherever You call me to do something, I realize it might not be easy—it could be a major decision or a difficult choice. I am likely to have hesitations that delay me from saying yes to Your calling. Uncertainties and questions fill my mind:

_____

_____

_____ .

Replace my hesitancy with the courage and strength to respond with "I will go."

Help me to trust in Your words in Deuteronomy 31:8: "The Lord himself goes before you and will be with you; he will never leave you nor forsake you. Do not be afraid; do not be discouraged." (Tell God about the encouragement you received from His words in the verse above.)

_____

_____

_____ .

I will be confident so I can step out with enthusiasm for what You want me to do now and in the future. Amen.

BEING SENT

So they sent their sister Rebekah on her way, along
with her nurse and Abraham's servant and his men.
And they blessed Rebekah and said to her, "Our sister,
may you increase to thousands upon thousands; may
your offspring possess the cities of their enemies."

GENESIS 24:59–60

Regardless of how Rebekah's family felt about Rebekah's
decision to leave immediately, they put aside their own
sentiments and gave Rebekah their blessing.

Rebekah's family prayed for God to show her favor
in her new life. They repeated a similar promise as that
given to Abraham: "I will surely bless you and make your
descendants as numerous as the stars in the sky and as the
sand on the seashore. Your descendants will take possession
of the cities of their enemies" (Genesis 22:17).

Rebekah would indeed play a part in God's promise to
Abraham. Rebekah was about to marry Isaac, the son given
to Abraham and Sarah. Isaac was the child through whom
Abraham's descendants would become as numerous as the
stars.[a] Through Isaac, God would fulfill His purpose of
filling the earth with His people. Through Abraham, Isaac,
and Jacob would come the people of Israel who would
possess the cities of their enemies when God brought them
back to Canaan to possess the land.

Rebekah's family prayed for God to show His favor
to Rebekah as she took her part in bringing about God's
promise.

It is important, as you step into God's purposes for

[a] But God said
to him, . . . "It is
through Isaac that
your offspring
will be reckoned"
(Genesis 21:12).

85

you, to bring other people alongside you. Find people not only with whom you can share what God is calling you to do, but who will enthusiastically support you and your decision. Ask them to pray for God's favor and blessing on you, to know His goodness, to receive His strength, and much more. Ask them to pray for God to work through you so other people can receive God's blessing.

Yesterday, you prayed to say, "I will go." Today, pray for God to make known people who can encourage, support, and pray for you as you step into God's purposes.

Lord God, I ask You to surround me with people who can encourage, support, and pray for me. I need others to come alongside me. Would You make it very clear who those people should be? Amen.

(As God gives you names of people who can come alongside you, write them down here.)

_____   _____

_____   _____

_____   _____

_____   _____

(Then reach out to them.)

DEPENDING ON GOD

Isaac was forty years old when he married Rebekah daughter of Bethuel the Aramean from Paddan Aram and sister of Laban the Aramean. Isaac prayed to the LORD on behalf of his wife, because she was childless. The LORD answered his prayer, and his wife Rebekah became pregnant.

GENESIS 25:20–21

Rebekah was childless.

Rebekah stepped into God's purpose for her life, to be the wife of Isaac. God's promise of numerous descendants would be fulfilled through Isaac and Rebekah. Rebekah's family had sent her to Isaac with a blessing to "increase to thousands upon thousands" (Genesis 24:60). Yet, Rebekah could not conceive.

Rebekah's story reminds us of Sarah. However, Rebekah's and Sarah's stories take different paths. Whereas Abram took Sarai's slave Hagar as his wife to have a child, Isaac "prayed to the LORD on behalf of his wife" (25:21). God answered his prayer.

As Rebekah struggled to conceive, we can encounter obstacles or difficulties even when we know we're doing what God has planned for us. When we are tempted to take matters into our own hands, Isaac reminds us to pray. It is so simple yet often so hard to leave our problems with God in prayer. We do not know whether our prayers will be answered in twenty minutes or twenty years. Rebekah and Isaac waited twenty years for a child.[a]

Although the Bible states simply that Isaac prayed and

[a] Isaac was sixty years old when Rebekah gave birth to them (Genesis 25:26).

his prayer was answered, the Hebrew word for *prayed* gives us a better perspective. The word means "to plead" or "supplicate," in other words to beg earnestly or humbly. Isaac prayed fervently.

When we pray, we can question if our prayers are making a difference. However, when we pray, we are doing our part while we are waiting on God to do His part. We pray persistently and passionately while trusting God's timing, however hard it is and however long it takes.

Pray using one or more of the Scripture passages below, sharing honestly with God about your experience of persisting in prayer and waiting on His timing and His ways.

Lord God, Your Word says: "The prayer of a righteous person is powerful and effective. Elijah was a human being, even as we are. He prayed earnestly that it would not rain, and it did not rain on the land for three and a half years. Again he prayed, and the heavens gave rain, and the earth produced its crops" (James 5:16–18). Sometimes I don't feel like my prayers are effective because

_____

_____ .

Encourage me to know that I don't need to be special, but that living right with You makes my prayers powerful. "Rejoice always, pray continually, give thanks in all circumstances; for this is God's will for you in Christ Jesus" (1 Thessalonians 5:16–18). Sometimes I give up and stop praying because

_____

_____ .

Encourage me to know that asking is what You want me to do. "Ask and it will be given to you; seek and you will find; knock and the door will be opened to you. For everyone who asks receives; the one who seeks finds; and to the one who knocks, the door will be opened " (Matthew 7:7–8). Sometimes I don't ask because

_____

_____ .

"Which of you, if your son asks for bread, will give him a stone? Or if he asks for a fish, will give him a snake? If you, then, though you are evil, know how to give good gifts to your children, how much more will your Father in heaven give good gifts to those who ask him!" (vv. 9–11). Sometimes I question if You will give me the good things I ask for because

_____

_____ .

Encourage me to expect the best from You. Amen.

ASKING GOD

The babies jostled each other within her, and she said, "Why is this happening to me?" So she went to inquire of the LORD.

GENESIS 25:22

God answered Isaac's prayer. Rebekah became pregnant. Then something felt amiss. Rebekah went to "inquire of the LORD" (Genesis 25:22). And God answered her question. The kicking she was experiencing was more than from carrying twins; the two boys were fighting for dominance that would be played out in life. Whereas normally the older child would be favored and receive twice the inheritance of the younger child,[a] in the case of these children, God foretold Rebekah that "two nations are in your womb, . . . one people will be stronger than the other, and the older will serve the younger" (Genesis 25:23). God's promise of His chosen descendants would continue through the younger son. God's choice can be hard to understand; we are never explicitly told why God chose to elevate Jacob over his twin brother.

a "Birthright refers to the right of the firstborn to inherit from the father twice as much as the younger brother or brothers will inherit."[1]

We too can face perplexing situations when something feels uneasy or not right. We too can ask ourselves, "Why is this happening to me?" Or we may see God's working out His ways that don't seem right or fair. We may not understand God's ways. His plans and purposes may not be what we expect or consider conventional. They may be perplexing or upsetting. But like Rebekah, we should talk to God and ask for His understanding.

Attentively watch and listen for God's guidance as you

ask Him to answer what is perplexing you. Remember God's Word says: "Do not be anxious about anything, but in every situation, by prayer and petition, with thanksgiving, present your requests to God. And the peace of God, which transcends all understanding, will guard your hearts and your minds in Christ Jesus" (Philippians 4:6–7).

Lord God, I come to You with the same question Rebekah asked: Why

_____

_____

_____

_____ ?

God, I ask for understanding of what is perplexing me and for Your guidance on how to respond. (Journal what God impresses on your heart and mind.)

_____

_____

_____

_____ .

No matter what, I ask You to fill my heart and mind with overwhelming peace like only You can give. Amen.

ZEAL FOR GOD'S PURPOSES

Now Rebekah was listening as Isaac spoke to his son Esau. When Esau left for the open country to hunt game and bring it back, Rebekah said to her son Jacob, "Look, I overheard your father say to your brother Esau, 'Bring me some game and prepare me some tasty food to eat, so that I may give you my blessing in the presence of the LORD before I die.' Now, my son, listen carefully and do what I tell you."

GENESIS 27:5–8

ebekah, so generous, hospitable, and enthusiastic. Suddenly, outright devious.

Esau was Isaac's favorite child.[a] As the oldest and as was customary, Esau should have received Isaac's blessing. Rebekah favored Jacob. Whatever Rebekah's reasons, her favoritism most likely influenced her devious plan to ensure Jacob received the blessing instead of Esau. She could have also wanted to make sure that God's revelation to her that "the older will serve the younger" came true (Genesis 25:23).

Rebekah worked behind the scenes devising a flawless plan to swindle Esau so Isaac blessed Jacob. Rebekah was so determined she took full responsibility, even willing to take the blame upon herself: "My son, let the curse fall on me. Just do what I say" (27:13). This time Rebekah's eagerness was misplaced. Perhaps zeal for God's purposes

[a] Isaac, who had a taste for wild game, loved Esau, but Rebekah loved Jacob (Genesis 25:28).

got the better of her. Yet God would bring about His purposes, though it might seem strange, through her devious plan.

Rebakah's behavior is a warning for us. We need to be aware of the influence we can have, particularly in our homes. We need to be careful that we don't take sides or pit one person against another.

In our eagerness, however well-intended, we must be careful not to aim to pull the strings, to overstep what God wants. We must be careful that partiality does not get the better of us.

God "delights in people who are trustworthy," says Proverbs 12:22. Let's be women who are honest and genuine in our dealings with others, but most of all, whose behavior is pleasing to God.

Lord God, grant me an awareness of the impact I have in my spheres of influence. (Make a list of all the people you have authority over, lead, or teach.)

_____

_____

_____ .

Where I have misled others, I ask for Your forgiveness. Forgive me for

_____

_____ .

Give me the wisdom to be honest and trustworthy in all I do (write down some areas of responsibility)—

_____

_____

_____

—so I am a delight to You. Amen.

LIVING WITH OUR MISTAKES

When Rebekah was told what her older son Esau had said, she sent for her younger son Jacob and said to him, "Your brother Esau is planning to avenge himself by killing you. Now then, my son, do what I say: Flee at once to my brother Laban in Harran. Stay with him for a while until your brother's fury subsides. When your brother is no longer angry with you and forgets what you did to him, I'll send word for you to come back from there. Why should I lose both of you in one day?"

GENESIS 27:42–45

Rebekah's plan worked. Jacob did indeed receive the blessing intended for his older brother, but not without devastating consequences. Isaac trembled violently either from shock or outrage, or both. Esau cried bitterly.[a] Once he realized Isaac's blessing given to Jacob could not be reversed, his distress turned to intense anger.[b] Rebekah's plan caused enormous angst in her family.

If Esau followed through on his threat to kill Jacob once Isaac died, Rebekah would lose her favorite son as well. The curse had indeed fallen on Rebekah. She had achieved her purpose at the cost of her family. So Rebekah devised another plan to keep Jacob safe by sending him to live with her family.

Rebekah's story started so well yet ended so devastatingly. We do not know if Rebekah ever saw Jacob again. We don't know if Rebekah was alive when Esau and Isaac eventually put their hostilities behind them some twenty

[a] Read Genesis 27:33–34.

[b] Esau held a grudge against Jacob because of the blessing his father had given him. He said to himself, "The days of mourning for my father are near; then I will kill my brother Jacob" (Genesis 27:41).

years later.[a] Generous and bighearted, she responded willingly to God's plan for her life. Her meddling, however, alienated all the people she loved. We sense the deep pain her actions brought on herself and Jacob, Esau, and Isaac. Rebekah's deviousness is the last we read about her.

It gives us food for thought as we conduct our lives and relationships.

We may not devise such devious plans as Rebekah, but we are aware that our words and actions often cause friction or long-term fractures with those we love. If there are any mistakes we have made and hurt we have caused, we are to remember that God's mercy and forgiveness are always available. And we should pray constantly for—and work toward—the healing of our broken relationships.

Let's be women who leave legacies of building relationships and not tearing them apart.

Lord God, where I have made mistakes or broken hearts in relationships, I ask for Your forgiveness and healing. Forgive me for

_____

_____ .

In particular, I ask You to let me know if I need to apologize, make amends, or do anything to bring about further reconciliation and restoration in that relationship. (Listen for God's response to your prayer, and write it down.)

_____

_____

_____ .

May I find rest knowing that nothing can stand in the way of Your plans and purposes. Amen.

[a] But Esau ran to meet Jacob and embraced him; he threw his arms around his neck and kissed him. And they wept (Genesis 33:4).

A WOMAN OF SORROW
Rachel

A WOMAN OVERLOOKED
Leah

Leah and Rachel are inseparable. Not only because they were sisters but because they were both married to the same man.

Rachel and Leah were the daughters of Laban, Rebekah's brother. Rebekah sent Jacob to live with Laban to escape Esau's threat to his life. There Jacob married both Leah and Rachel. Leah and Rachel's relationship is dominated by love, jealousy, and rivalry. Yet we discover in the middle of their intense dealings with each other that God is faithful. He is compassionate, caring, and constant because of His promise made to Abraham, passed on to Isaac and to Jacob, and also to these two women.

CONTENT WITH YOURSELF

> Now Laban had two daughters; the name of the older
> was Leah, and the name of the younger was Rachel.
> Leah had weak eyes, but Rachel had a lovely figure
> and was beautiful.
>
> GENESIS 29:16–17

W e are introduced to the two daughters of Laban by a comparison of their physical features. Rachel is described as "beautiful" and having "a lovely figure" (Genesis 29:17). With Leah, we are left wondering what it meant to have "weak eyes" (v. 17). Even biblical scholars are uncertain. But one thing we can be sure about, Rachel had beauty. Leah did not.

The biblical comparison of Rachel and Leah is unsettling. We know that beauty is more than physical appearance. Inner beauty is important, "the unfading beauty of a gentle and quiet spirit, which is of great worth in God's sight" (1 Peter 3:4). There is more to a person than their outward appearance. God, we are told, considers our hearts more than what we look like.[a]

Reading about Rachel can make us feel uncomfortable about ourselves and our bodies. We compare what we look like to the description of Rachel, even though we have no details, and can feel dissatisfied with the width of our hips, the length of our legs, the texture of our hair. Rachel is described in a way we know most of us are not. We can find ourselves envious of her beauty, even though

[a] The LORD does not look at the things people look at. People look at the outward appearance, but the LORD looks at the heart (1 Samuel 16:7).

it is in God's Word. It's a feeling we don't expect to have when we read the Bible. It seems wrong.

Whether we compare our bodies or any of our other qualities with other people, comparison can lead to a range of emotions: resentment or contentment, jealousy or pride, feelings of worthiness or unworthiness, feeling a fraud, vulnerable, frustrated and more.

Not only do we end up disliking or criticizing ourselves when we make comparisons, but we assess other people on their outward appearance too. We decide whether we like them or not. We decide if they are worthy or unworthy of our friendship. We have probably made a decision whether we would be friends with Rachel or Leah.

As we look at the lives of Rachel and Leah, let's begin by knowing that thinking negatively about ourselves or being dismissive of other people is not honoring to God. He has formed each one of us to look the way we do, whether we like it or not. He does, however, care more about the integrity of our hearts.

Heavenly Father, I must admit I can be dissatisfied with the way I look. I find it hard to be content with

———————————————————————————————— .

At the same time, I want to be grateful and enjoy the way You have designed me. I give You praise for the physical abilities and personality traits that You have given me. In particular, I thank You for

———————————————————————————————— .

———————————————————————————————— .

Free me up to celebrate Your handiwork and gifts. And help me to be less preoccupied about my physical attractiveness and more attentive to the condition of my heart. Amen.

BEING LOVED

Jacob was in love with Rachel and said, "I'll work for you seven years in return for your younger daughter Rachel." Laban said, "It's better that I give her to you than to some other man. Stay here with me." So Jacob served seven years to get Rachel, but they seemed like only a few days to him because of his love for her.

GENESIS 29:18–20

Rachel was not only beautiful, but she was deeply and passionately loved by Jacob. We may wonder if Jacob loved Rachel only because she was beautiful. Jacob's love for Rachel was so fierce he was willing to wait seven years for Rachel's hand in marriage.

Unlike Abraham who sent his servant laden with gifts in exchange for Rebekah's prompt marriage to Isaac (Genesis 24:53), Jacob had no such wealth. So Jacob ended up working for his uncle for a marriage settlement instead. Laban was indifferent toward Jacob and unsentimental about his love for Rachel. No recognition of Jacob's love was taken into account.

When we read of Jacob's love for Rachel, we see an example of persevering love. Jacob waited and waited to marry Rachel. Then when the day finally came, he was deceived into marrying Leah and not Rachel, and had to agree to work for another seven years to be able to marry Rachel as well.[a]

We all long to be loved with such persevering love. You may have a devoted spouse who has shown you love and

[a] Read Genesis 29:26–27.

tenderness for many years, and so you know love like this. Perhaps you are in a new relationship and hoping that love will last.

Although we may struggle to know long-lasting human love, we do have a God who loves us with unfailing love. Psalm 33:5 says, "The earth is full of his unfailing love." This means you cannot miss out on God's love. You are surrounded by His love each and every moment of the day and night. It is God's unfailing love that protects you, rescues you, and means He never takes His eyes off you.

Pray about the human love you know or need, but also ask God that you would know His endless love. Use the words of Psalm 143:8 as your prayer: "Let the morning bring me word of your unfailing love, for I have put my trust in you."

Lord God, thank You that I cannot miss out on Your love. Thank You for the reminder that Your love surrounds me like (put in your own words how you picture God's love encompassing you)

_____

_____ .

I also thank You for the people in my life who have shown and show me love

_____

_____ .

At the same time, I want to be loved (write down the ways in which you want to receive love)

_____

_____

_____ .

As I put my trust in You, each morning may I be reminded of Your endless love for me. Amen.

UNLOVED

Then Jacob said to Laban, "Give me my wife. My time is completed, and I want to make love to her." So Laban brought together all the people of the place and gave a feast. But when evening came, he took his daughter Leah and brought her to Jacob, and Jacob made love to her. And Laban gave his servant Zilpah to his daughter as her attendant. When morning came, there was Leah! So Jacob said to Laban, "What is this you have done to me? I served you for Rachel, didn't I? Why have you deceived me?"

GENESIS 29:21–25

Leah wasn't just part of Laban's deceptive plan; she was the reason for his plan. Laban wanted his older daughter married, loved or not.

We do not know what Laban told Leah that led her to stand next to Jacob on that wedding day instead of Rachel. We do know, however, that Leah, intentional or not, gave Jacob the mistaken impression that she was Rachel. We sense that as well as being part of the deception of Jacob, Leah was also a victim. We wonder how Leah with her weak eyes could have been taken for Rachel with her lovely figure, but most likely Leah was veiled on her wedding day.

Laban viewed marriage as a necessity rather than taking anyone's feelings into consideration. And Jacob, with his outburst, was just as insensitive toward Leah.

Jacob did not love Leah. He loved Rachel. So, a week later he married Rachel as well, in agreement with Laban for another seven years of work.

Suddenly, Leah found herself in a marriage in which her husband loved her beautiful sister. Leah was in a complicated relationship that would be the soil for much friction.

Relationships today can be similarly complicated. You may know the pain and sorrow of what it is to be unloved. You may also know what it's like for the person you love to love someone else.

When we feel unloved, we are to remember that God also knows what it is like to be unloved. These words from Hosea give a picture of God's broken heart when the people He loved no longer loved Him: "When Israel was a child, I loved him, and out of Egypt I called my son. But the more they were called, the more they went away from me. . . . It was I who taught Ephraim to walk, taking them by the arms; but they did not realize it was I who healed them. I led them with cords of human kindness, with ties of love. To them I was like one who lifts a little child to the cheek, and I bent down to feed them" (Hosea 11:1–4).

Talk to God about your pain of being unloved and the heartache of complicated relationships.

Lord God, thank You for understanding my desire to be loved or to have my love returned. Being unloved makes me feel

---

When the relationships I cherish are difficult and complicated, it makes me feel and react

---

Comfort me with Your love. Where my heart has been broken, heal it with Your love. Amen.

GOD'S UNFAILING LOVE

When the LORD saw that Leah was not loved, he enabled her to conceive, but Rachel remained childless. Leah became pregnant and gave birth to a son. She named him Reuben, for she said, "It is because the LORD has seen my misery. Surely my husband will love me now."

GENESIS 29:31–32

Leah's longing to be loved by Jacob led to intense heartache. The Bible describes it as *misery* (Genesis 29:32). It is the same Hebrew word used to describe Hagar's misery, meaning to "crouch" or "hunch up." It's like Leah's heart and confidence shriveled with the lack of love.

Leah felt sure that giving Jacob a son would change his desire for her. After son number three she said, "Now at last my husband will become attached to me, because I have borne him three sons" (Genesis 29:34). Yet Jacob's feelings remained indifferent toward her. *Attached* means to "join oneself." It reminds us of the words "become one flesh" used by God to describe the marriage relationship in Genesis 2:24.[a] Jacob and Leah's marriage, however, lacked oneness. Their feelings were not the same for each other.

But God *saw* that Leah was not loved, just as God saw and heard Hagar's misery (day 22). And as Hagar knew God saw her, Leah knew God saw her wretchedness and heard her cries (Genesis 29:32).

In His compassion for her loveless marriage, God gave Leah children. Bearing children may not have compensated for the misery of being unloved by her husband, but her

[a] That is why a man leaves his father and mother and is united to his wife, and they become one flesh (Genesis 2:24).

pregnancies made her aware of God's love. By the time she gave birth to her fourth son, she was able to say, "This time I will praise the LORD" (29:35).

The longing to be loved by someone who doesn't love us may never be fixed. But we can be reassured that God sees our ongoing heartache. He hears the constant cries of our hearts.

When you don't know human love, reflect on God's unfailing love in the Scripture verses below so you can praise Him.

Lord God, I thank You and praise You for Your dependable, round-the-clock love. (Read the following verses and then praise God in your own words.)

"I will be glad and rejoice in your unfailing love, for you have seen my troubles, and you care about the anguish of my soul" (Psalm 31:7 NLT). I praise You for

_____

_____ .

"When I said, 'My foot is slipping,' your unfailing love, LORD, supported me" (Psalm 94:18). I praise You for

_____

_____ .

"Do not remember the sins of my youth and my rebellious ways; according to your love remember me, for you, LORD, are good" (Psalm 25:7). I praise You for

_____

_____ .

Amen.

JEALOUSY

When Rachel saw that she was not bearing Jacob any children, she became jealous of her sister. So she said to Jacob, "Give me children, or I'll die!" Jacob became angry with her and said, "Am I in the place of God, who has kept you from having children?"

GENESIS 30:1–2

Each month reminded Rachel she could not get pregnant. Eventually, Rachel reached a breaking point. However, it wasn't just her inability to conceive that made her disgruntled; it was because of Leah's ability to pop out one baby after another. The scourge of barrenness left Rachel more than disappointed and distressed; it grew into an ugly envy of her sister. She resented Leah for her fertility in comparison to her infertility.

Rachel made irrational demands on her husband—"Give me children, or I'll die!" (Genesis 30:1)—knowing perfectly well he wasn't at fault. His children with Leah were proof. Only God, pointed out Jacob in a vehement retort, could fulfill Rachel's request.

We've seen the pain of not getting pregnant and the need to do something about it with Sarah and Rebekah. Rebekah's husband prayed to God. Sarah resorted to the culturally accepted practice of surrogacy, having a child by means of a servant or slave. Rachel took the same route. "Here is Bilhah, my servant," she said to Jacob. "Sleep with her so that she can bear children for me and I too can build a family through her" (v. 3).

When Rachel's servant Bilhah gave birth to a son, Rachel said, "God has vindicated me" (v. 6). She acknowledged that God had listened to her plea. But instead of praising God for giving her a child, and clearing her name of shame, she saw God's answer as a way to triumph over her sister: "I have had a great struggle with my sister, and I have won" (v. 8).

When someone has achieved or gotten something that we want, we too can be jealous. Jealousy makes us say things to hurt the other person. We behave unreasonably and unkindly. We are mean instead of generous. We can also take the good things God has given us, through answered prayer or even just from His goodness to us, and use them to get back at another person.

Ask God to show you where you are letting jealousy cause you to say or do things that are wrong.

Lord God, as I take time to pause before You, I ask You to show me where I am letting jealousy get the better of me in my relationships either at home, at work, or with friends. (Sit before God and let Him show you where you have been resentful, angry, defensive, irrational, mistrustful . . . Then ask Him for forgiveness.)

Forgive me for saying

_____

_____ .

Forgive me for doing

_____

_____ .

Show me where and how I need to make amends. (Write down what God brings to mind.)

_____

_____

_____ .

Amen.

BEING SATISFIED

When Leah saw that she had stopped having children,
she took her servant Zilpah and gave her to Jacob as
a wife. Leah's servant Zilpah bore Jacob a son. Then
Leah said, "What good fortune!" So she named him
Gad. Leah's servant Zilpah bore Jacob a second son.
Then Leah said, "How happy I am! The women will
call me happy." So she named him Asher.

GENESIS 30:9–13

Leah no longer obsessed over winning the love of her
husband; she also vied for superiority over her sister in
having children. Rachel and Sarah bore children by their
servants because they had no children. Leah had given birth
to four sons. Still, when she couldn't get pregnant again,
she also resorted to using her servant. Giving birth became
a competition with Rachel and earning prestige among the
women in their community. "How happy I am! The women
will call me happy" (Genesis 30:13), said Leah when her
servant Zilpah gave birth to her second son, Asher.

With the birth of her first four children, Leah cried out
to God and eventually praised Him for His goodness. She
realized God had seen her misery and heard her cries. Then,
the meaning of the names of her children acknowledged
the actions of God: Reuben—the Lord has seen my misery; Simeon—the Lord heard; and Judah—praise the Lord
(29:32–35).

No longer did Leah cry out to or praise God. The meanings of the names of her children borne by her servant
Zilpah were unconnected to the work of God. The name

[a] "Gad (*găd*) = Personal name meaning 'good fortune.'"[1]

[b] "Asher (*ash'-ur*) = Fortunate; happy. Fortress."[2]

Gad means "good fortune,"[a] and the name *Asher* means the same thing or "happy."[b] Their meanings are unlike her gratitude for being seen and heard by God. Their names are associated with Canaanite deities (for example, the name Asher is likely connected with the name of the Canaanite goddess Asherah or that of the Assyrian god Ashur) rather than the one true God.[3]

How easy it is to forget the good things God has given us when our eyes are diverted to compare what we haven't got with what other people have got. Even when God has shown His love and answered our prayers abundantly, we can still want more.

Take a few moments to think about what God has given you, how He has shown His love to you, and thank Him.

Heavenly Father, I thank You for showing me Your love in giving me so many good things. (List everything that is good in your life, as many as space allows.)

_____

_____

_____ .

Forgive me for being dissatisfied with

_____

_____

_____ .

Forgive me when I forget all that You have given me and want more. Amen.

DAY 41

OUT OF CONTROL

During wheat harvest, Reuben went out into the
fields and found some mandrake plants, which he
brought to his mother Leah. Rachel said to Leah,
"Please give me some of your son's mandrakes."
But she said to her, "Wasn't it enough that you took
away my husband? Will you take my son's mandrakes
too?" "Very well," Rachel said, "he can sleep with
you tonight in return for your son's mandrakes."

GENESIS 30:14–15

Leah and Rachel resorted to superstition. Mandrakes
were believed to have aphrodisiac qualities or increase
fertility.[a]

Rachel could not bear the thought of Leah having an
advantage over her regarding fertility. Leah couldn't bear
Rachel having the upper hand in her marriage. Leah seemed
to spit out her questions as statements. Rachel had stolen
her husband. Rachel wanted to steal a chance at increased
fertility too. Yet Leah was willing to trade the mandrakes
for a night with Jacob. Together, Rachel and Leah turned
their husband into an object sold at the lowest price: "'Very
well,' Rachel said, 'he can sleep with you tonight in return
for your son's mandrakes'" (Genesis 30:15).

Desperation displaced any affection Leah had for Jacob.
"'You must sleep with me,' she said. 'I have hired you
with my son's mandrakes'" (v. 16). The two sisters made
a contract for their husband's services.

It's easy to look at Leah and Rachel and think we
would never let jealousy get the better of us or let it get

[a] "Sometimes called
a 'love apple,' it was
purported to be an
aphrodisiac and en-
hancer of fertility."[4]

111

so ridiculously out of control. Yet often we let our feeling of bitterness or resentment run freely in our minds. We let our jealous thoughts dictate our behaviors. We stop giving compliments or praise. We overemphasize our own achievements. We make snide comments.

Intentional or not, other people, including children, can get dragged into our green-eyed conflicts.

The Bible says: "For wherever there is jealousy and selfish ambition, there you will find disorder and evil of every kind" (James 3:16 NLT). Even in our pain and grief, let's not give our jealousy and selfish ambition free rein. Instead, let's turn to God so our conflicts don't get out of control.

Let's practice getting on our knees and pouring out our problems to God. Then we will receive wisdom from God that "is first of all pure; then peace-loving, considerate, submissive, full of mercy and good fruit, impartial and sincere" (James 3:17).

(Write down an attribute of God's wisdom from James 3:17, shown above, that stands out to you.) Lord God, the wisdom You give is

_____ .

I know Your wisdom is always available when I need it. I ask You to give me wisdom in all my relationships, to be peace-loving, gentle, and open to reason. (Write down those relationships that are most important to you.)

_____

_____

_____ .

Amen.

GOD WHO GIVES GRACIOUSLY

God listened to Leah, and she became pregnant and bore Jacob a fifth son. Then Leah said, "God has rewarded me for giving my servant to my husband." So she named him Issachar. Leah conceived again and bore Jacob a sixth son. Then Leah said, "God has presented me with a precious gift. This time my husband will treat me with honor, because I have borne him six sons." So she named him Zebulun.

GENESIS 30:17–20

God in His tenderheartedness listened to Leah and enabled her to get pregnant again. And Leah realized it. God did what the mandrakes could not do.

Leah saw the birth of her next two children as gifts from God. God was good to Leah. Throughout her loveless marriage, God loved Leah. While she pined for the affection of her husband, God showed her His love. During the time she could get pregnant, and the time she could not get pregnant, God was with her. During the time she kept her eyes on God, and during the time she saw only the struggle and conflict with her sister, God still saw her.

As we have seen with Hagar, we can be confident that God sees and hears us when we are downtrodden and unloved. God is faithful to us even when we put faith in the things around us rather than in Him. Even though we are imperfect in our thoughts, words, and behaviors, God still gives good gifts to us.

The truth is, we are flawed in our thinking. We crave the love of people more than the love of God. We ask for what we want more than desiring God's will. We try to control the events of our lives instead of letting God decide. We are imperfect people with imperfect motives and yet in the middle of our mess, God is gracious to us. Let's thank God for His good gifts and His tenderheartedness toward us.

Heavenly Father, I thank You that I am Your child, and that You shower me with Your goodness, no matter how imperfect I am. I want to remember and reflect on seasons of my life when I powerfully experienced Your faithfulness and graciousness. (Identify and express thanks to God for times in which God's gifts were particularly evident.)

_____

_____

_____

_____

_____ .

In my life right now, I give You thanks for the gifts of

_____

_____

_____ .

Thank You also for the gift of Your grace, and the life given to me through Your Son, Jesus. Amen.

GOD WHO REMEMBERS

Then God remembered Rachel; he listened to her and enabled her to conceive. She became pregnant and gave birth to a son and said, "God has taken away my disgrace." She named him Joseph, and said, "May the LORD add to me another son."

GENESIS 30:22–24

God "remembered" Rachel (Genesis 30:22).

God had not been so focused on Leah that He had no concern for Rachel. Rachel was equally deserving of God's attention. God wasn't absent-minded or just not paying attention. The word *remembered* is used elsewhere in the Bible to refer to God's faithfulness to His covenants and promises. The promise that God had made to Abraham and Sarah continued to Jacob. God promised Abraham, Isaac, and then Jacob that *He* would cause them to be fruitful and multiply. Just as God came to Sarah in His timing, so God remembered Rachel in His timing. God was gracious and compassionate to Rachel as He was to Leah.

After the pain of childbirth, Rachel made a statement filled with the recognition of what God has done for us: "God has taken away my disgrace" (v. 23). God had removed the shame of being childless. God had filled the gap that led to the friction and fighting with her sister. God had completed the one thing missing in her marriage. Rachel recognized God was awesome and powerful.

We can be assured that the God who sees and hears also remembers us. He is faithful to us.

If God listened to Hagar, a woman unseen and neglected by those entrusted with caring for her—then He listens to you. If God loved Leah, an overlooked and unloved woman, then He loves you too. If God remembered a heartbroken and disgraced woman named Rachel, then He remembers you too.

When God *remembers*, circumstances change, and we change too. God becomes bigger in our lives. We become more aware of His awesomeness.

Psalm 36:5 (NLT) says, "Your unfailing love, O LORD, is as vast as the heavens; your faithfulness reaches beyond the clouds." If we are in any doubt over how God treats us, then Psalm 86:15 (NLT) is a reminder: "But you, O Lord, are a God of compassion and mercy, slow to get angry and filled with unfailing love and faithfulness."

We can get frustrated that God takes so long to remember, to show His faithfulness to us. When we are waiting for Him to answer specific requests, let's look for His love and faithfulness to us in every situation and every moment of the day. Pray to know God's faithfulness to you.

Lord God, I am reminded of Your awesome love and faithfulness already shown to me and how You have remembered me. (Paraphrase what you wrote yesterday, on Day 42, and praise God again.)

_____

_____

_____ .

As I wait for You to answer my request of

_____

_____

_____ ,

I will remember You *are a God of compassion and mercy, slow to get angry and filled with unfailing love and faithfulness.* Amen.

GOD'S OVERARCHING PURPOSE

Then Rachel and Leah replied, "Do we still have any share in the inheritance of our father's estate? Does he not regard us as foreigners? Not only has he sold us, but he has used up what was paid for us. Surely all the wealth that God took away from our father belongs to us and our children. So do whatever God has told you."

GENESIS 31:14–16

Rachel and Leah are finally in agreement. After all the squabbling and fighting with each other, they both realize they have been taken advantage of by their father. They are in agreement with their husband too. God told Jacob the time had come for him to return to Canaan. Rachel and Leah were happy for this to happen. This sudden reversal in the way they responded to each other seems remarkable.

For years Rachel and Leah jockeyed for dominance in their marriage and predominance over one another in their childbearing. These battles became insignificant when they compared it to the unfair treatment at the hands of their father.

Laban had been indifferent toward them the moment he had given them away in marriage. For fourteen years their husband had worked for his father-in-law in return for his marriage to Rachel. Jacob had helped build the fortunes of Laban, yet Rachel and Leah had gained nothing.

Daughters never expected to receive the same inheritance as sons, but Rachel and Leah lamented their unfair treatment was worse than expected.

We've been in the nitty-gritty with Rachel and Leah, in the ups and downs of their lives, but for a moment, we remember the bigger picture. God was at work to bring about His promise, given first to Abraham, to

Isaac, and then to Jacob—that of descendants and land. God's promise to Jacob still stood.ᵃ

Often it's good for us to be reminded of God's broader purposes for ourselves and for those around us. We can get so caught up in the day-to-day details of our lives that we forget God's overarching purpose to give us a future with Him: "He gave his one and only Son, so that everyone who believes in him will not perish but have eternal life. God sent his Son into the world not to judge the world, but to save the world through him" (John 3:16–17 NLT).

Being reminded of God's broader purposes can put our own complaints into perspective. Pray over what you need to let go of as you remember God's purpose for yourself and others in your life.

Lord God, I ask You to give me a greater awareness of Your good plans and purposes. (Reflect on the following verses and then pray about the frustrations and complaints you need to let go of.)

"For God so loved the world that he gave his one and only Son, that whoever believes in him shall not perish but have eternal life" (John 3:16).

"God our Savior, who wants all people to be saved and to come to a knowledge of the truth" (1 Timothy 2:3–4).

Forgive me for my frustrations with

_____ .

Forgive me for my complaints about

_____ .

Give me Your perspective and fill me with Your peace as I go about my day. Amen.

MAKING MISTAKES

When Laban had gone to shear his sheep, Rachel stole her father's household gods.

GENESIS 31:19

Perhaps Rachel could not get beyond the fact that Laban had robbed her and Leah of their happiness, even though God had "remembered" her and God was with Jacob, Rachel, and Leah. God had not allowed Laban to harm them. God had taken away Laban's livestock and given it to Jacob.[a]

[a] Read Genesis 31:4–9.

Still, Rachel stole what was valuable to her father, the household gods. The Hebrew word for *steal* can also mean "deceive." Rachel deceived her father as he had deceived her and Leah in their marriage. Perhaps Rachel decided to get revenge on her father for treating her unfairly. It was petty retaliation against her father.

The decision to steal could have been a rash act in the heat of the moment when her emotions were running high. Or it could have been a cold, deviously thought-out decision. Whichever it was, the consequences would have turned out the same.

Jacob was so sure that no one in his household, let alone his beloved wife, would have stolen the gods that he pronounced death for that person: "But if you find anyone who has your gods, that person shall not live" (Genesis 31:32). Rachel had even deceived the man who loved her.

Perhaps Rachel decided she had made a silly mistake. Or maybe she didn't realize her small act would have such huge consequences. Rachel had the weight of deception

119

and the weight of the figurines to contend with and hide. We don't know how Rachel continued to hide the objects. Or whether she disposed of them. We don't know if they were ever found, if the truth ever came out.

Anything we do that is wrong, however small and insignificant it seems at the time, has consequences. Even if we didn't intend to harm anyone, what we do affects those around us.

Maybe you have done something to get back at a person who has hurt you. Or maybe you did something years ago that you now realize was a silly mistake, but the thought of being found out still haunts you.

Let's ask God for forgiveness for the wrongs we have committed. Let's also be women who do not retaliate or aim to get revenge.

Lord God, by Your very nature, You are truth. In our world where there is so much deceit, I want to be a woman who is known for her truthfulness.

Where I have misled others for my own gain, forgive me. Where I have led another person to believe something that is not true, forgive me. Where I have

_____

_____ ,

forgive me. Teach me Your truth. (Write down the areas in your life where you want to be honest and sincere.)

_____

_____ .

Give me the wisdom to focus on what You have done for me, not on what other people have done to me. Amen.

A WOMAN OF SORROW

> Then they moved on from Bethel. While they were still some distance from Ephrath, Rachel began to give birth and had great difficulty. And as she was having great difficulty in childbirth, the midwife said to her, "Don't despair, for you have another son." As she breathed her last—for she was dying—she named her son Ben-Oni. But his father named him Benjamin. So Rachel died and was buried on the way to Ephrath (that is, Bethlehem).
>
> GENESIS 35:16–19

We come to the end of Rachel's life. At the birth of Joseph, Rachel prayed for God to give her another child.[a] But the joy of giving birth to another son turned to sorrow when Rachel realized she would die.

Ben-Oni, meaning the "son of my sorrow."[b] We grieve with Rachel. In delivering the second child she wanted so much, she did not get to enjoy him or see him grow up.

Rachel's life is a tapestry of sorrows. The heartache of infertility. The pain of seeing her sister give birth so easily. The sadness of being at the mercy of her father's unscrupulous behavior. Then the sorrow of not knowing her second child. Yet, in her sorrow, Rachel is able to be a comfort to those who are sorrowful.

Rachel is depicted as weeping bitterly when the Israelites were taken into exile. "A voice is heard in Ramah, mourning and great weeping, Rachel weeping for her children and refusing to be comforted, because they are no more" (Jeremiah 31:15). It was appropriate for Rachel to weep

[a] She named him Joseph, and said, "May the LORD add to me another son" (Genesis 30:24).

[b] "His father, Jacob, changed his name from *Ben-Oni* ('son of my sorrow') to *Benjamin* ('son of my right hand')."[5]

because the Israelites were her children. She and Leah were the mothers of the twelve tribes of Israel.

However, God speaks hope to Rachel and all those who are mourning: "'Do not weep any longer, for I will reward you,' says the LORD. 'Your children will come back to you from the distant land of the enemy'" (Jeremiah 31:16 NLT).

Perhaps you can relate to Rachel. Your life has been one of complexity and sadness. You mourn what you have lost. You are reminded daily of what is no more. When you see or hear of others who have experienced sorrow like yourself, you mourn for them and with them. You too can be a comfort to those who know tragedy and sorrow.

The words in Jeremiah are for you too. In the middle of sorrow and pain, God says there is hope for the future. What we have experienced will not be in vain. One day there will be "'no more death' or mourning or crying or pain" (Revelation 21:4). Until that time, place your hope in God.

The same God who was with Rachel is with you. God also speaks these words to you: "Blessed are those whose help is the God of Jacob, whose hope is in the LORD their God" (Psalm 146:5). Pray to be a woman who places her hope in God.

Lord God, I lay before You my pain and my grief:

Show me that my suffering has not been in vain. Renew my hope in You for the future.

(Reflect on the following Scripture passage and then ask God to renew your hope in the ways you need.) "But those who hope in the LORD will renew their strength. They will soar on wings like eagles; they will run and not grow weary, they will walk and not be faint" (Isaiah 40:31). As I wait for You, Lord, I am counting on You to

_____

_____

_____ .

May the hope You give me enable me to be a comfort to those who need hope. Amen.

FINDING SIGNIFICANCE

> Then he gave them these instructions: "I am about to
> be gathered to my people. Bury me with my fathers
> in the cave in the field of Ephron the Hittite, the cave
> in the field of Machpelah, near Mamre in Canaan,
> which Abraham bought along with the field as a
> burial place from Ephron the Hittite. There Abraham
> and his wife Sarah were buried, there Isaac and his
> wife Rebekah were buried, and there I buried Leah."
>
> GENESIS 49:29–31

Jacob, at the time of his death, gave instructions to his sons that he should be buried with his ancestors. In this instruction, we discover that Jacob would lie alongside Leah. Leah was together with Jacob in death as she had not been in life. Leah, unloved but who yearned to be loved by her husband, had her resting place alongside the man by whom she longed to be recognized. A woman and wife who always took second place finally took precedence. What Leah wanted in life she got in death.

Leah also earned significance, alongside Rachel, in that their children headed up the twelve tribes of Israel. Leah had the honor of being the mother of two of the most significant tribes in the history of Israel. The tribe of Levi became the tribe of the priesthood. The tribe of Judah became the tribe of royalty through whom came David, Solomon, and also Jesus.[a]

Leah may have been overlooked by her husband, but Leah was not overlooked by God. God saw Leah.

You are seen by God. God loves you. You are not

[a] This is the genealogy of Jesus the Messiah the son of David, the son of Abraham: Abraham was the father of Isaac, Isaac the father of Jacob, Jacob the father of Judah and his brothers (Matthew 1:1–2).

overlooked by Him. Rest in the assurance that however insignificant you feel, you are of value and significance to God.

We may never stop wanting and needing to be loved by another human being. But, at the same time, let's not miss out on how God is good to us. Let's not be so preoccupied with wanting human acceptance and love that we miss noticing God's love.

We may know our significance to God in our lifetime; on the other hand—like Leah—we may not know this side of eternity the full significance of what we do. We should, however, live confidently, assured that we have a role to play in God's purposes.

Lord God, I turn my eyes to focus on Your goodness, graciousness, and the love You give me. As I commit to putting my trust and hope in You, assure me in all my circumstances that I can find rest in You. (List the circumstances where you need God-given confidence.)

_____

_____

_____

Thank You for the significance I find in You. While I long to be significant to others, may I find satisfaction in You. (Sit in God's presence and ask Him to share His love and care for You; journal about the experience.)

_____

_____

_____

Amen.

A WOMAN IN THE BACKGROUND
Jochebed

Jochebed's name is not familiar to us. Her actions, however, are well known. Jochebed hid her baby in a basket on the river Nile. She is the mother of Moses.

History had moved on since the time of Rachel and Leah. Rachel and Leah gave Jacob twelve sons who would become the twelve tribes of Israel. Leah's sons sold Joseph, Rachel's eldest son, into slavery. God, however, was with Joseph. He rose to the highest position in Egypt next to Pharaoh. Because of Joseph, Jacob, now called *Israel*, and his eleven sons were able to settle in Egypt and escape the famine in Canaan.[a]

[a] Read Genesis 47:5–6.

After Joseph died, the Israelites continued to live in Egypt. They were "exceedingly fruitful" and "multiplied greatly," just as God promised (read Exodus 1:6–7). Jochebed was one of these Israelites. Jochebed teaches us that even if we are in the background, we can still be significant in playing a part in God's purposes.

DAY 48

UNNOTICED

Now a man of the tribe of Levi married a Levite
woman . . .

EXODUS 2:1

This Levite woman is not named. And in being unnamed,
she is barely noticed. We learn her name elsewhere, in
Exodus 6:20, where she is identified as *Jochebed*, married
to Amran from the clans of Levi. Levi was the third son
born to Leah.

Jochebed's name is also mentioned in Numbers 26:59,
where we are told she gave birth to three remarkable people.[a]
Moses, the greatest leader of the Israelites; Aaron, appointed
by God to assist Moses in the exodus from Egypt and
Israel's first high priest; and Miriam, a prophet, musician,
and leader whom we will learn about beginning on day 53.

In the shadow of three significant and godly leaders,
Jochebed remained in the background. Yet we have to
believe that Jochebed played a significant role in how
Moses, Aaron, and Miriam grew to be God-fearing leaders.

We know that motherhood is a critical and vital role in
the development of children. Yet often the responsibilities
can go unnoticed or can be undervalued. Raising children,
whether our own or others', is often hard work with few
accolades. Instead, our culture commends achievements in
professional work and even praises roles in ministry before
motherhood. Or we applaud fame and prominence, from
celebrities to the number of likes or followers we have on
social media. We may aspire to be mothers, but we do not
desire to be in the background.

[a] The name of
Amram's wife was
Jochebed, a descen-
dant of Levi, who
was born to the Le-
vites in Egypt. To
Amram she bore
Aaron, Moses and
their sister Miriam
(Numbers 26:59).

The Bible teaches that we are not to seek or be preoccupied with status and recognition, but are instead to be childlike. Jesus said, "Whoever takes the lowly position of this child is the greatest in the kingdom of heaven" (Matthew 18:4). This doesn't preclude us from using our wisdom, discernment and God-given judgment in all our activities, but we are to recognize our positions in relation to God's greatness, to look to Him for all we are and do, like a child looks to and depends on a mother.

Let's pray, whatever our positions, to recognize and be content with where God is calling us, whether that is in the spotlight or in the background. May we find in God our full worth without needing a sense of self-importance, trusting and believing in where He has us and finding courage for what He wants us to do.

Lord God, give me the wisdom to know I am significant to You, in who I am and what I do, whether You are inviting me to be behind the scenes or at center stage, whether my role is seemingly ordinary or extraordinary. (Write down the roles that you have, noting whether they are, in your eyes, in the foreground or background, ordinary or impressive.)

_____

_____

_____

Help me to resist the temptation of finding my worth in the opinions of other people or through the standards of the world around me. May I have a childlike trust in You and confidence in my significance to You, where You have me, and what You want me to do. I look to You for wisdom and discernment in my roles. I will depend on You for my worth. (Tell God the ways in which you can show your dependence on Him.)

_____

_____

_____

Amen.

SEEING SIGNIFICANCE

And she became pregnant and gave birth to a son. When she saw that
he was a fine child, she hid him for three months.

EXODUS 2:2

Jochebed lived at a risky time to be pregnant.

Circumstances had changed for the Israelites since Joseph was in
power. Pharaoh and the generations of Joseph and his brothers died. The
new king of Egypt felt threatened by the population growth of the Israelites.
He reduced the Israelites to a life of slavery in order to curb their growth
and instructed that all Israelite baby boys be killed at birth. Pharaoh's
instruction went unheeded by the Hebrew midwives, and so he instructed
all Egyptian people to throw any Israelite baby boy into the Nile.

Jochebed lived within the confines of slavery and the fear of losing her
baby. Motherly instincts and something special about her little boy made
her desperate to keep her baby alive.

Perhaps Jochebed noticed her baby was strong and healthy, or maybe
in the depths of her soul she knew this baby would be remarkable in some
way, that God had a special future for him.

Significance is not just about ourselves; it is seeing significance in others.
In particular, we have a responsibility of giving attention to and investing
in the next generation.

Every person and child is important enough for us to fret over and be
concerned about the dangers and challenges they encounter. Every person
and child should be destined for a life filled with good things and to know
the goodness of God.

Let's be women who help each other see our worth, particularly our
importance to God instead of focusing on our own importance. Let's bring
out the strength and beauty in each other, and let's pour into those who are
younger, who have been given to us by God.

Lord God, help me to have an outward focus and to recognize the significance and worth in other people.

(Fill in the following prompts with names of people in your life, those who God brings to your mind.)

May I share with _____
that they are worthy of Your love.

May I see the strength and beauty in _____ ,
and share with them their value.

May I teach, train, or mentor _____ ,
who are younger or more inexperienced than I am, to be the best they can be in life. Amen.

DOING WHAT YOU CAN

But when she could hide him no longer, she got a papyrus basket for him and coated it with tar and pitch. Then she placed the child in it and put it among the reeds along the bank of the Nile. His sister stood at a distance to see what would happen to him.

Exodus 2:3–4

Jochebed came up with a plan to protect and preserve the life of her baby. Fingers blackened with tar, Jochebed painted a basket to make it waterproof and to protect her son from getting wet, or the basket filling with water and sinking. With the baby inside, she waded into the water and placed the basket among the reeds. There, in the quieter waters, her baby would be protected from the current and the risk of floating downstream. In the river and not at home, he would be away from the inquiring ears and prying eyes of her Egyptian neighbors. Jochebed protected her baby in a place no one would have thought to look, the river Nile where Hebrew babies were being drowned.

Jochebed did what she could to save her child. We can wonder, though, how she thought this solution would save him in the days or weeks ahead, or give her child a life expectancy to adulthood.

At the same time she was doing all she could, Jochebed needed faith that God would do what only He could do and safeguard her son.

We too may do all we can for the people we care about, the people we just prayed for on Day 49 to know their significance and worth. Often it never feels like enough, and it is not enough. Even though our purposes are good, we still fret over whether we could have done more.

We do what is humanly possible, but we have to trust that God can do more than we can. The people we care for and pray for are also God's concern.

Our well-intentioned plans and good concerns pale in comparison to

God's goodness and what He knows is good and needed for each person. We often think of what is important and valuable in human terms, but God is able to think of what is perfectly good.

Yesterday we prayed to help others know their significance. As we do our part, let's pray for God to do His part.

Lord God, what I do for the people I love and care about can never be enough. And rightly so. Today, I ask You to do what I cannot do. (Fill in the prompts with the names of people God brings to your mind; these may be the same people you prayed for yesterday or different people.)

Shower Your kindness and goodness on

_____ .

Provide for the needs of

_____ .

Protect and care for

_____ .

Amen.

ONLY GOD

Then Pharaoh's daughter went down to the Nile to bathe, and her attendants were walking along the riverbank. She saw the basket among the reeds and sent her female slave to get it. She opened it and saw the baby. He was crying, and she felt sorry for him. "This is one of the Hebrew babies," she said. . . . Pharaoh's daughter said to her, "Take this baby and nurse him for me, and I will pay you." So the woman took the baby and nursed him. When the child grew older, she took him to Pharaoh's daughter and he became her son. She named him Moses, saying, "I drew him out of the water."

EXODUS 2:5–6, 9–10

God did His part as only He could. God did what Jochebed could not do. Pharaoh's daughter, a woman in close contact with the man who gave the command to kill Jochebed's baby, rescued the child. An Egyptian who had been ordered to take Moses's life, gave him life. Moses would live in the palace with the man who had only human power to kill him, but God used His almighty power to preserve Moses's life.

What joy Jochebed must have known to learn from her daughter that her baby's life was secure through a formal arrangement with the princess. Not only that but Moses would be returned to her until he was weaned. God's goodness didn't stop there. Jochebed, a slave woman, would receive payment for bringing up her own child.

Jochebed had time to love and nurture Moses during that time of weaning, and to do all that she could to teach him about the God of their forefathers and foremothers and the promises He made to His people.

Jochebed must have poured everything she had, every waking moment, into her child for those precious years. Although heart-wrenching to give him up to be raised as Egyptian royalty and to be schooled in Egyptian ways and religion, she could believe that she had done a good job. God would be with Moses.

We often say, "Let go and let God," and when we do, we get the opportunity to see God work in amazing and remarkable ways. We can place our trust in God for those we care about, and not underestimate the goodness and power of God Almighty, and what He can do for them.

Whatever you are worried about for those you love, remember that whatever dangers and challenges they face, what people intend for evil God can work for good.[a] And whatever time you have been given to pour into and pray for the next generation, whether an hour or years, is both precious and worthwhile.

Let's be women who do what we can and pray in every way we can in the background and let God Almighty do His part in the foreground.

Lord God, I praise You because You are great. Your power is limitless. Your wisdom is more than I can comprehend. I praise You because You work in amazing and remarkable ways.

I ask, believing in faith, that You can *do immeasurably more than all we ask or imagine, according to Your power that is at work within us.* (Review who and what you prayed for on days 49 and 50. Now make your prayers bigger and bolder.) I ask for

_____

_____

_____

_____

Let me see You work in ways I have not expected so I can be amazed and praise You even more. Amen.

[a] You intended to harm me, but God intended it for good to accomplish what is now being done, the saving of many lives (Genesis 50:20).

DAY 52

FAITH NOT FEAR

By faith Moses' parents hid him for three months after he was born, because they saw he was no ordinary child, and they were not afraid of the king's edict.

HEBREWS 11:23

Jochebed, though unnamed in Hebrews 11:23, gets her recognition as a woman of great faith. She is listed among the other great men and women of faith, next to her son Moses.

Jochebed's story told in two hundred and fifty words in the Bible seems unimportant. Her trust in God is behind the scenes. Yet her act of faith played an important part in God's plan to use her son to deliver His people from slavery in Egypt.

The Bible does not give Jochebed an opportunity to speak about her faith, but her actions speak louder than words. Hiding Moses was not done out of fear of Pharaoh; it was done because she had confidence in God. Jochebed believed that in doing her part, God would do His part in preserving the life of her son.

We have to think that her faith influenced Moses's faith in God. Just as she was "not afraid of the king's edict" (Hebrews 11:23), the Bible says of Moses: "By faith he left Egypt, not fearing the king's anger" (v. 27).

We should be impressed and encouraged by this ordinary woman. What makes Jochebed more remarkable is that she was an enslaved woman, ineffectual against a cruel dictator. However, God worked in His power through Jochebed's courage, and the courage of her two sons Moses and Aaron, to overcome the powers of Egypt.

We do not need to have a prominent role, or be in a position of authority in our world to make a difference. We just need faith in God who is all-powerful. Courageous dependence on God is unseen work that leads to amazing outcomes.

Faith means not giving in to the fears we encounter. Faith means believing God is greater than the fears that overshadow us. Jochebed chose faith, not fear. You too can choose faith, not fear.

Let's be women who are concerned for the people and children in our lives not because we are fearful of what they come up against, but because we have faith that God can do far more than we ask or imagine. Then perhaps one day we'll see in them the same faith we have shared with them.

Lord God, whether my roles are in the background or the spotlight, it is my faith in You that is most important. I am believing that "Ah, Sovereign, LORD, you have made the heavens and the earth by your great power and outstretched arm. Nothing is too hard for you" (Jeremiah 32:17).

Now that I know it is Your power at work through me, I ask to have faith in You to _____ ,

not give into the fear of _____ ,

to see those I love and care about as _____
and to have a strong faith in You. Amen.

A WOMAN
LEARNING HUMILITY
Miriam

Miriam grew up as a slave. She lived in Egypt toward the end of the four hundred years that the Israelites were enslaved and mistreated. Miriam's story in the Bible begins when she is watching over her brother Moses, placed in the river Nile by his mother in order to preserve his life. In her life, Miriam experienced God's miraculous deliverance of His people from the hands of the Egyptians. The remainder of her life, however, was spent wandering in the wilderness with the Israelites.

Miriam is the sister of Moses, a man of great significance. Miriam had significance too. She was a leader of the Israelites alongside her two brothers, Moses and Aaron.

We will discover that Miriam was a woman who learned humility the hard way. Her lesson is one from which we can learn because God approves of the attribute of humility.

TAKING ON RESPONSIBILITY

His sister stood at a distance to see what would happen to him. Then Pharaoh's daughter went down to the Nile to bathe, and her attendants were walking along the riverbank. She saw the basket among the reeds and sent her female slave to get it. She opened it and saw the baby. He was crying, and she felt sorry for him. "This is one of the Hebrew babies," she said. Then his sister asked Pharaoh's daughter, "Shall I go and get one of the Hebrew women to nurse the baby for you?" "Yes, go," she answered. So the girl went and got the baby's mother.

EXODUS 2:4–8

We are introduced to Miriam as she watched over her baby brother placed in a basket in the river Nile by her mother.

Miriam was probably in her early teens. The word *girl* used here in Hebrew means a female of marriageable age. Miriam was certainly old enough to stay by herself and watch over the baby. She was also old enough to think for herself and respond wisely to Pharaoh's daughter.

It is nearly impossible that Jochebed could have anticipated the scenario that unfolded with Pharaoh's daughter. Instead, Miriam showed great initiative in suggesting a wet nurse for her baby brother, and good sense in keeping silent when proposing her own mother.

We can ponder what it was like to be the older sister of both Moses and Aaron. (Exodus 7:7 tells us Aaron was three years older than Moses.) We may wonder or even know what it is like to be given huge responsibility when we are young, like having to watch over a younger brother.

Maybe you can relate to being the eldest child with younger siblings. Perhaps as the oldest daughter you have been given adult tasks by your mother or parents. Perhaps you have enjoyed or resented taking on responsibility, emulating the role of a mother.

Maybe you are a younger sibling, and even in adulthood, you are parented by an older sibling, either appreciating it or seeing it as unfair or unhealthy. Even being an only child comes with great responsibility and pressure.

Thinking about the position we hold in our families can stir up mixed emotions. Bring any unresolved emotions to God, your heavenly Father, and ask Him to give you peace and understanding regarding your family.

Heavenly Father, when I think about my position within my family, I feel

_____

_____

_____

Give me a greater appreciation of my place within my family.

With those I am related to by birth, marriage, or adoption, I ask for the wisdom to

_____

_____

_____

I ask for peace as

_____

_____

Amen.

BEING A LEADER

Then Miriam the prophet, Aaron's sister, took a timbrel in her hand, and all the women followed her, with timbrels and dancing. Miriam sang to them: "Sing to the LORD, for he is highly exalted. Both horse and driver he has hurled into the sea."

EXODUS 15:20–21

Leadership, it seems, came later in life for Miriam. It is eighty or more years since Miriam watched over her baby brother on the bank of the river Nile.[a] Miriam is now a much older woman.

[a] Read Acts 7:20–30.

In that time, Miriam had been called by God to be a prophet. She is among only a small number of women named as prophets in the Bible. Miriam had also become a leader of the Israelites alongside her two brothers, Moses and Aaron.[b]

[b] I brought you up out of Egypt and redeemed you from the land of slavery. I sent Moses to lead you, also Aaron and Miriam (Micah 6:4).

Miriam had other leadership roles too, as a musician, singer, and worship leader. She could dance too. All the women of Israel followed Miriam's lead. She taught them the song that Moses had written.[c] This song explained the greatness and goodness of God who had rescued His people from the bitter hardship of slavery, miraculously parted the Red Sea, and destroyed their enemies who had oppressed them for four hundred years.

[c] "This 'Song of the Sea' probably was the earliest-authored portion of the book of Exodus. Moses apparently composed it immediately after the deliverance that it describes (15:1)."[1]

Miriam had a prominent position given to her by God as a prophet and leader among the Israelites.

Like Miriam, you may hold a prominent leadership position. God has gifted you with specific talents, vision, and discernment to inspire the direction of a company, initiative, or ministry. Or, perhaps, you don't lead in an official capacity. Leadership is not just about holding high-profile positions; all of us lead in some way. We have responsibility, influence, guide, inspire confidence, convince other people to follow us, and more. There are many definitions of leadership. We can be leaders whatever our age, status, or ability.

One aspect of leadership mentioned in the Bible is that we are to lead with a modest self-perception of ourselves, to be willing to prioritize the needs of others. Jesus is the model leader for us in this aspect. Another aspect of leadership is that we are to look to God and Jesus and submit to His leadership.

Take a moment to think about where you lead and your area of God-given prominence. Pray to have humility and to be led by God.

Lord God, thank You for the opportunity to be a leader. (Write down the areas where you influence, guide, inspire confidence, have followers, have responsibility.)

_____

_____

_____ .

(Read the wisdom in these verses and then tell God how you can give glory and honor to Him in the way you lead.)

"Trust in the LORD with all your heart; do not depend on your own understanding. Seek his will in all you do, and he will show you which path to take. Don't be impressed with your own wisdom. . . . Instead, fear the LORD and turn away from evil. Then you will have healing for your body and strength for your bones" (Proverbs 3:5–8 NLT).

I will give honor and glory to You in the way I lead by

_____

_____ .

Being a leader

I will prioritize the needs of others by

_____ .

I commit to Your leadership over my life by

_____ .

Amen.

OVERSTEPPING OUR ROLES

Miriam and Aaron began to talk against Moses because of his Cushite wife, for he had married a Cushite. "Has the LORD spoken only through Moses?" they asked. "Hasn't he also spoken through us?" And the LORD heard this.

NUMBERS 12:1–2

In yesterday's reading, Miriam used her role as a worship leader to help the women give glory to God. In today's reading, we see a completely different leader, one who is a critical older sister and disgruntled partner dragging her brother into complaining with her.

Arrogance is the word that comes to mind with Miriam's complaints. She had an exaggerated sense of her own importance and an opinion about her brother's personal decisions which were not hers to have. Moses, deeply humble, was undeserving of her complaining.[a] Moses had the very quality that is required of a leader in God's eyes.

[a] Read Numbers 12:3.

It is so easy to be critical of other people, especially those within our families. It's often the ones we love the most that we think we should correct the most. We think our siblings or other family members should know better. We hold them to higher standards than other people. On one hand, we are right to be concerned about the decisions of a loved one. On the other hand, their decisions are not ours to make.

It is also particularly easy to be critical when we are

strong leaders. We see where other leaders go wrong. We see where we could do better. We get envious of another person's higher or more influential position, thinking we deserve to be where he or she is. Or we let pride seep in, thinking more of who we are and what we have achieved. There is nothing wrong with ambition and being competitive but when we let pride and arrogance take over, we are in the wrong.

Let's be women who are aware of our criticism of others and particularly our arrogance or pride as leaders or as family members. Let's ask God for forgiveness.

Lord God, I come before You asking for You to be merciful to me.

(Read the following verses and then ask God for His forgiveness.)

"Do not let any unwholesome talk come out of your mouths, but only what is helpful for building others up according to their needs, that it may benefit those who listen" (Ephesians 4:29). Forgive me for

_____

_____ .

"Do not seek revenge or bear a grudge against anyone among your people, but love your neighbor as yourself. I am the LORD" (Leviticus 19:18). Forgive me for

_____

_____ .

"Look beneath the surface so you can judge correctly" (John 7:24 NLT). Forgive me for

_____

_____ .

"[Love is not] rude. It does not demand its own way. It is not irritable, and it keeps no record of being wronged" (1 Corinthians 13:5 NLT). Forgive me for

_____

_____ .

Amen.

REALIZING WRONGDOING

At once the LORD said to Moses, Aaron and Miriam, "Come out to the tent of meeting, all three of you." So the three of them went out. Then the LORD came down in a pillar of cloud; he stood at the entrance to the tent and summoned Aaron and Miriam. When the two of them stepped forward, he said, "Listen to my words."

NUMBERS 12:4–6

Miriam and Aaron's complaint against Moses received a swift response from God: "When there is a prophet among you, I, the LORD, reveal myself to them in visions, I speak to them in dreams. But this is not true of my servant Moses; he is faithful in all my house. With him I speak face to face, clearly and not in riddles; he sees the form of the LORD" (Numbers 12:6–8).

As a prophet, Miriam knew God spoke to her through visions and dreams. However, God spoke directly and distinctly to Moses. Moses was unique in his relationship with God, "whom the LORD knew face to face" (Deuteronomy 34:10). God called him "my servant" (Numbers 12:7). And Moses was special to God because he was faithful and trustworthy to God.

Miriam learned something in that encounter with God. Miriam's complaint wasn't just against Moses; it was against God. And in their criticism of Moses, Miriam and Aaron had aroused God's anger.[a] Miriam's discontent with Moses

[a] Read Numbers 12:8–9.

had questioned God Himself. Miriam and Aaron should have been hesitant, not quick, to speak against Moses, God's leader and special servant.

Yesterday, on day 55, we brought our discontent to God. This was the correct response, and we should do so in all humility before God. When we are tempted to grumble and complain about other leaders, we are to remember they have been appointed or placed there by God. This applies to those in church leadership as well as the leaders of governments.[a]

While providing honest criticism and holding leaders accountable for their actions are crucial elements to any healthy institution, gossip and grumbling are displeasing to God. Where we have complained about those in leadership, particularly within the church, and where we feel that submitting to governing authorities is not something we should have to do, let's ask God for forgiveness.

Lord God, I again ask for Your forgiveness. Where I have complained about leadership at church or work by

_____

_____ ,

show me Your mercy. Where I have criticized those in leadership in my country by

_____

_____ ,

show me how I can pray for them instead.

(Spend a few moments thinking about the instructions of 1 Timothy 2:1–2 [NLT]: "I urge you, first of all, to pray for all people. Ask God to help them; intercede on their behalf, and give thanks for them. Pray this way for kings and all

[a] Everyone must submit to governing authorities. For all authority comes from God, and those in positions of authority have been placed there by God (Romans 13:1 NLT).

who are in authority so that we can live peaceful and quiet lives marked by godliness and dignity." Then in your own words pray for someone in authority.) Lord God,

_____

_____

_____ .

Amen.

GOD'S GRACIOUSNESS

When the cloud lifted from above the tent, Miriam's skin was leprous—it became as white as snow. Aaron turned toward her and saw that she had a defiling skin disease, and he said to Moses, "Please, my lord, I ask you not to hold against us the sin we have so foolishly committed. Do not let her be like a stillborn infant coming from its mother's womb with its flesh half eaten away." So Moses cried out to the LORD, "Please, God, heal her!"

NUMBERS 12:10–13

When God left them, to the shock and horror of Aaron and Moses, God had inflicted Miriam with leprosy. Aaron immediately recognized that he and Miriam had been foolish and sinned. Aaron's request for forgiveness, "I ask you not to hold against us the sin we have so foolishly committed" (Numbers 12:11), is a humble prayer that we should emulate. Moses graciously interceded with God on behalf of Miriam.

God's punishment of Miriam seems harsh. We can wonder why Aaron was not also punished. Miriam, however, mentioned first when she and Aaron spoke against Moses, seemed to have been the instigator. God's punishment seems severe. But on other occasions when the Israelites sinned against God and experienced God's anger, they did not live.[a] Miriam's punishment lasted for only seven days.[b]

Our tendency when reading this part of Miriam's story can be to focus on the anger of God and the punishment Miriam received. God's anger is frightening and hard

[a] Read Numbers 11:1.

[b] Confine her outside the camp for seven days; after that she can be brought back (Numbers 12:14).

152

to understand. We can wonder if illnesses or natural disasters are God's punishment on us.

Although God's anger is part of His holy character because He cannot tolerate sin, we have to remember that God is slow to anger. God says about Himself, "The LORD, the LORD, the compassionate and gracious God, slow to anger, abounding in love and faithfulness" (Exodus 34:6), and that "he relents from sending calamity" (Joel 2:13).

Jesus began His ministry by saying that He had been sent by God "to proclaim the year of the Lord's favor" (Luke 4:19). We live in the time of God's goodness and grace. Jesus took God's anger and punishment upon Himself so that we can enjoy God's kindness.

Jesus healed those who were sick, and when His disciples asked if a man's blindness was the result of his sin or his parents' sin, Jesus replied, "Neither this man nor his parents sinned" (John 9:3).

Instead of being fearful of God's anger, we are to dwell on His mercy, kindness, and favor shown to us.

Lord God, You are (name an attribute of God's that you appreciate)

_____

_____ .

Today, I ask You to give me a greater understanding of Your abundant mercy and grace. Sometimes I still fear that You view me in this unfavorable light:

_____

_____ .

But I know that Jesus, Your Son, took all my sin upon Himself so that I might enjoy Your favor. Thank You that having faith in Your Son frees me from any fear. Amen.

REMEMBERED WELL

In the first month the whole Israelite community arrived at the Desert of Zin, and they stayed at Kadesh. There Miriam died and was buried.

NUMBERS 20:1

From the generation of people who escaped Egypt, Miriam is the only woman to have her death recorded in the Bible. Miriam died in the wilderness. Miriam, along with Moses and Aaron, led a faithless generation who were more fearful of God than bold enough to have faith in God's goodness to enter the land He had given them. Neither Miriam nor Moses and Aaron got to enter into the land God promised them either.

Miriam had the privilege of playing a role in saving God's servant Moses as a baby. She served alongside two of Israel's greatest leaders. She had a special place in Moses's heart shown when he made his compassionate plea to God to heal her from leprosy.

We are not told if Miriam married or had children, even though this would have been customary for a woman. God chose Miriam to be His prophet and leader, and she had this honor as an older woman.

Although Miriam is recognized for many good things, she learned a hard lesson about gossiping and grumbling, jealousy and pride. The last recorded incident with Miriam is when she angered God and He inflicted her with leprosy. Yet her punishment was short-lived. We can imagine that Miriam learned to think a lot less of herself during those seven days inflicted with a disease that made her an outcast.

We can learn from Miriam about having an accurate and balanced understanding of ourselves and who we are in relation to God. Humility means being comfortable with our positions and letting others be a step ahead. Humility means treating others with respect and dignity, and not being self-seeking.

Humility is the proper relationship we should have with God. It requires us to reflect on who we are in relation to God, to accept God's discipline, and to be willing to grow in all areas of our faith. James 4:10 (NLT) says, "Humble yourselves before the Lord, and he will lift you up in honor." Whatever our roles as leaders, big or small, let's remember they are given to us by God.

Let's pray to be women who are reverential before God and respectful with one another.

Lord God, I come before You in humility. (Take a posture before God that will reflect your humility.) Cultivate in me an understanding of who You want me to be. Nurture in me an understanding of how You want me to follow You in everything I do. (Tell God what you've learned from the devotions about Miriam about the posture of your heart before Him.)

Guide me in what is right and instruct me in Your way.[a] *Most of all teach me that humility begins with my reverence for You.*[b] *Amen.*

[a] He leads the humble in doing right, teaching them his way (Psalm 25:9 NLT).

[b] Humility is the fear of the LORD (Proverbs 22:4).

A WOMAN OF FAITH AND ACTION
Rahab

Rahab was a prostitute. Rahab lived in Jericho, an ancient heavily fortified city in the land of Canaan, the land that was promised by God to Abraham and the Israelites. God had commanded Joshua to cross over the river Jordan and conquer Canaan. Joshua had targeted Jericho as his first conquest.

Prostitution would have placed Rahab in the lowest classes of society. However, we are to remember that prostitution does not mean exclusion from being in the family of God. Jesus welcomed prostitutes and others who were on the edges of society. They were more eager to believe in Him than the religious leaders.[a]

Rahab had a remarkable faith in God Almighty that she put into action. From her, we will discover that faith and action go together.

[a] [Jesus said,] "I tell you the truth, corrupt tax collectors and prostitutes will get into the Kingdom of God before you do" (Matthew 21:31 NLT).

OVERCOMING LABELS

Then Joshua son of Nun secretly sent two spies from Shittim. "Go, look over the land," he said, "especially Jericho." So they went and entered the house of a prostitute named Rahab and stayed there.

JOSHUA 2:1

Rahab's home would have been a suitable location for the spies to enter Jericho unsuspected. Two men entering and leaving Rahab's home under the guise of being her clients would not have drawn attention.

In naming Rahab's profession, we are told something about her status. Rahab lived an immoral life and had a low position in society at that time. It could be said the same of prostitutes today.

Naming her with her profession brings to the forefront an uncomfortable reality we deal with today. People are often labeled. Names are applied to people that don't fully or correctly represent who they are. Labels are often restrictive and inaccurate.

Maybe you are labeled an introvert, disabled, divorced, and as much as you'd like to, you can't move beyond how people see you. Perhaps you label yourself—a failure, undeserving, or ugly.

Labels limit our ability to find out more about people, and to think about them or ourselves differently. When we label ourselves, we stop ourselves from moving beyond what we have been or who we think we are.

When we think about labels in relation to God, we don't allow ourselves to see other people as God sees them, and we don't allow ourselves to believe the truths that God speaks about us.

God looks beyond labels. God wants us to be the people He intends us to be. You are not stuck with your labels.

However insignificant you feel, however undervalued you perceive that you are, this does not exclude you from God's plans and purposes.

As we begin the story of Rahab the prostitute, let's bring the labels we stick to ourselves, and the words and phrases other people use to describe us, to God in prayer. Let's pray to be freed from the restrictive ways we are thought of and think about ourselves. Let's pray to have a greater understanding of how God sees us.

Lord God, this is how other people label me:

_____

_____ .

This is how it makes me feel:

_____

_____ .

These are the labels I stick to myself that make me feel uncomfortable and keep me stuck:

_____

_____ .

I ask You to free me from these labels and give me a new understanding of my value and worth in Your eyes. Amen.

MAKING A CHOICE

But the woman had taken the two men and hidden them. She said, "Yes, the men came to me, but I did not know where they had come from. At dusk, when it was time to close the city gate, they left. I don't know which way they went. Go after them quickly. You may catch up with them." (But she had taken them up to the roof and hidden them under the stalks of flax she had laid out on the roof.)

JOSHUA 2:4–6

When the spies turned up at Rahab's house, she had a choice. She could either hand them in or hide them. It seems Rahab had already made a decision over what she would do—Rahab "had taken the two men and hidden them" (Joshua 2:4)—by the time the king of Jericho's messengers arrived at her door and said, "Bring out the men who came to you and entered your house, because they have come to spy out the whole land" (v. 3).

Rahab chose to defy the demand of the king. She decided to save the lives of the enemy and side with the Israelites. Not only did Rahab choose to hide the spies, but she lied to her fellow countrymen about knowing who they were and their whereabouts. She sent the king's messengers on a fruitless pursuit in the wrong direction.

Although we don't know at this point how Rahab made those choices, her actions bring up an important question for us. How do we make choices? Or more importantly, how do we make wise choices?

The Bible assures us that "the fear of the LORD is the beginning of wisdom" (Psalm 111:10). Being in awe of God and having a deep respect for Him are where making good choices begin. If we are in any doubt about God or following God's wisdom, we can be assured that "the foolishness of God is wiser than human wisdom" (1 Corinthians 1:25), not that God is foolish. We can also be assured that what might look like good choices to everyone around us does not necessarily mean they are wise choices in

God's eyes: "the wisdom of this world is foolishness in God's sight" (1 Corinthians 3:19).

Let's be women who always ask God for His wisdom when making difficult and challenging choices. James 1:5 reassures us that "if any of you lacks wisdom, you should ask God, who gives generously to all without finding fault, and it will be given to you." There is no better reassurance than the promise in that verse.

Lord God, whatever choices I make, I am reminded that to make a wise choice, I can look to You and Your Word and ask for Your wisdom.

These are the difficult and challenging choices I face today:

_____

_____

_____ .

As I spend these few moments with You, I ask You to direct me, and show me the decisions that are wise. Remind me that the decisions that are pleasing to You are not necessarily the decisions that looks wise to those around me.

These are the actions I believe you are telling me to make. (Write down your decisions from the choices above.)

_____

_____

_____ .

Thank You for being generous with Your wisdom. Amen.

IN AWE OF GOD

For the LORD your God is God in heaven above and
on the earth below.

JOSHUA 2:11

We now have understanding for Rahab's choice to defy
her countrymen and hide the spies. Rahab had made
her decision based on what she knew about God and His
actions for His people.

The Israelites, although ordinary people like Rahab
and her people, were extraordinary because they had the
almighty God on their side. Rahab and the people of Jericho were terrified of the Israelites. She said: "I know that
the LORD has given you this land and that a great fear of
you has fallen on us, so that all who live in this country
are melting in fear because of you. We have heard how the
LORD dried up the water of the Red Sea for you when you
came out of Egypt, and what you did to Sihon and Og,
the two kings of the Amorites east of the Jordan, whom
you completely destroyed. When we heard of it, our hearts
melted in fear and everyone's courage failed because of
you" (Joshua 2:9–11).

The Red Sea had been no barrier to the Israelites escaping
Egypt. The Jordan River, a much smaller stretch of water,
even in its flood stage, would be no obstacle to the Israelites
about to advance on Jericho in their thousands from the
plains of Moab across the Jordan River.[a] The neighboring
kings of Sihon and Og had attacked the Israelites instead
of letting them pass through their territories. As a conse-
quence, they had been annihilated.

[a] Read Joshua
3:15–16.

Recounting the Israelite victory, Moses said, "The LORD our God also gave into our hands Og king of Bashan and all his army. We struck them down, leaving no survivors" (Deuteronomy 3:3).

Fate awaited the people of Jericho.

Rahab's fear, though, was in awe of God's strength and power. God Almighty would not fail to do everything that He promised His people, and that promise was "the LORD has given you this land" (Joshua 2:9).

Rahab stood out among her countrymen for her personal belief in the almighty God.

Our choice to believe in God is personal too. Trusting in God may mean standing out as different in your group of friends. It can mean being the first one in your family to make a decision to have faith in God. It may mean being one among thousands of people. Even if you made a personal decision to trust in God many years ago, restate your trust in God today.

Almighty God, I believe You are God of the heavens above and God over all the earth. In my own words, I believe You are (write down who God is to you)

_____

_____

_____

_____

_____

Amen.

DAY 62
ACTS OF KINDNESS

Now then, please swear to me by the LORD that you will show kindness
to my family, because I have shown kindness to you.

JOSHUA 2:12

We discover another layer to Rahab's decision to hide the spies. In
choosing to have faith in God Almighty and to be on the side of the
Israelites, Rahab chose to show kindness.

As the enemy, Rahab showed unexpected mercy to two men that would
have huge repercussions both for her own people and for the Israelites.
Her deed led to devastating consequences for the people of Jericho but a
successful mission for Joshua. Rahab's decision enabled the Israelites to
complete the first conquest of the land God had promised to them. Rahab
was a woman without a position in society of power or influence, yet her
act of kindness contributed to God's purposes and plans.

Rahab's generosity came with serious danger. She risked being discovered
as a traitor to her own people. More so, she risked losing her life, and the
lives of her family, when the Israelites attacked Jericho. So she needed the
spies to promise they would respond in kind.

Our acts of kindness can make a difference too. One small kindness
today can transform a person's life for tomorrow and the future.

Some acts of goodwill are easy and simple. Other times, kindness comes
with the risk or a cost to ourselves. We don't often ask for a guarantee that
our good deeds are reciprocated.

We may not know the outcome of our generosity. However, we can be
sure that no acts of kindness are in vain. God will be able to use them for
His glory. Through our acts of kindness, God's power is released so we and
others can be in awe of the amazing things that He can do.

Lord God, help me understand that my acts of kindness are never wasted but can be used by You for Your glory.

These are the small and easy ways I realize I can be kind:

_____

_____

_____ .

These are the harder, more costly ways I realize I can be generous:

_____

_____

_____ .

May Your power be released through my acts of kindness and generosity. May your purposes and plans be fulfilled through the goodwill I show to others. Amen.

GOD'S KINDNESS

"Our lives for your lives!" the men assured her. "If you don't tell what we are doing, we will treat you kindly and faithfully when the LORD gives us the land."

JOSHUA 2:14

Rahab requested that in return for her kindness, the spies would show compassion on her and her family: "Give me a sure sign that you will spare the lives of my father and mother, my brothers and sisters, and all who belong to them—and that you will save us from death" (Joshua 2:12–13).

The men made an oath, a binding promise, that her life and the lives of her family would be spared. For the oath to be binding, Rahab had to tie a scarlet cord from her window, bring her family members into her house, and not tell anyone about the plan.[a]

It would have been easy for Joshua and the spies to forget about their commitment to Rahab. Days and days passed between Rahab's request and the heat of the battle. The Israelites in their thousands had to cross the Jordan River. Every male Israelite had to be circumcised as commanded by God. Then for another six days the Israelites marched around the city of Jericho.

Yet Joshua and the spies did not forget their commitment to Rahab. Her life and the lives of her family were saved. Not only that, but Rahab found a home in the community of the Israelites under the protection of "the LORD your

[a] Read Joshua 2:17–20.

167

God [who] is God in heaven above and on the earth below" (2:11). Rahab recognized the power of kindness.

The Hebrew word for kindness, *hesed*, encompasses many meanings. It can mean "compassion," "forgiveness," "patience," "tenderness," "generosity," "mercy" and "grace." In Scripture, it refers to the way people treat each other. But it is most commonly used for God's actions toward us.

Rahab was shown remarkable kindness in return for her kindness. God shows extraordinary kindness to us too, except God's kindness is not based on anything we have done.

Maybe it's been a while since you've thought about the mercy, compassion, forgiveness, patience, and generosity of God. Jesus is the sure sign and oath that God's kindness is continuous and constant each day, spares us from death, and gives us new life for eternity.

God declares this about Himself: "I am the LORD, who exercises kindness, justice and righteousness on earth, for in these I delight" (Jeremiah 9:24). Thank God for His kindness.

Lord God, thank You for Your overwhelming kindness shown to me. (Recount several ways God has demonstrated His mercy and goodness to you personally.)

_____

_____

_____ .

Thank You for the sure sign of Jesus, Your Son, that reassures me of life. Thank You that when I ask, You always respond with compassion, mercy, patience, tenderness, and more. Today, I ask You show me Your kindness by

_____

_____

_____ .

Amen.

SAVING FAITH

By faith the prostitute Rahab, because she welcomed the spies, was not killed with those who were disobedient.

HEBREWS 11:31

Whatever Rahab's past or background, her faith elevated her to be listed among the great men and women of faith in the Bible. By believing and acknowledging "the LORD your God is God in heaven above and on the earth below" (Joshua 2:11), Rahab is commended for her faith in Hebrews 11 alongside Abraham, Sarah, Moses, and his parents.

Instead of being fearful of God like her fellow citizens, Rahab was in awe of God, which placed her with the people of faith. Faith saved her from death. Although Rahab, as a Canaanite, was an enemy of the Israelites, her faith saved her life and gave her a home in the camp of the Israelites for the remainder of her life. Galatians 3:7 says, "Those who have faith are children of Abraham." Rahab became a child of Abraham because of her faith.

Faith placed Rahab the prostitute in the genealogy of Jesus too. Rahab married an Israelite named Salmon and gave birth to Boaz who married Ruth. Boaz and Ruth had a son called Obed who was the grandfather of King David.[a] Jesus is from the lineage of King David.

Faith saved Rahab's life. Faith gave Rahab a future.

Rahab's faith story is also a beautiful example of what God does for those who are deemed insignificant and undervalued.

[a] Read Matthew 1:1–16.

169

Faith gives you life too. Faith removes the restrictive ways you think about yourself. You may be struggling to throw off the labels that others have placed on you or the way you think about yourself, but the Bible reassures us that "anyone who trusts in him will never be disgraced" (Romans 10:11 NLT).

Your faith includes you in God's family, in the promise given to Abraham and Sarah to have children as numerous as the stars. Galatians 3:29 (NLT) says, "Now that you belong to Christ, you are the true children of Abraham. You are his heirs, and God's promise to Abraham belongs to you." Even though you may feel like an outsider, or that your past labels you, faith gives you a home as God's child.

Lord God, thank You that faith in You frees me from the labels that say I am insignificant and unworthy. Instead of believing the labels other people put on me and the labels I stick on myself, I will believe what You say about me.

(Read the following verses and thank God in your own words for the significance and worth He gives you.)

"So God created mankind in his own image, in the image of God he created them; male and female he created them" (Genesis 1:27). Thank You for

_____

_____

_____ .

"And even the very hairs of your head are all numbered" (Matthew 10:30). Thank You for

_____

_____

_____ .

"You know the generous grace of our Lord Jesus Christ. Though he was rich, yet for your sakes he became poor, so that by his poverty he could make you rich" (2 Corinthians 8:9 NLT). Thank You for

_____

_____

_____ .

"But God demonstrates his own love for us in this: While we were still sinners, Christ died for us" (Romans 5:8). Thank You for

_____

_____

_____ .

Thank You that my faith places me in Your family with Rahab and all other women of faith. Amen.

FAITH IN ACTION

You see that a person is considered righteous by what they do and not by faith alone. In the same way, was not even Rahab the prostitute considered righteous for what she did when she gave lodging to the spies and sent them off in a different direction?

JAMES 2:24–25

Faith is not just what we believe; it is what we do.

Rahab's example of faith, believing and doing, is given alongside Abraham's faith: "Was not our father Abraham considered righteous for what he did when he offered his son Isaac on the altar? You see that his faith and his actions were working together, and his faith was made complete by what he did" (James 2:21–22).

Rahab is in stark contrast to Abraham. Abraham was the ultimate insider: God called him, spoke to him directly, and gave him the promise that would change the trajectory of humanity. On the other hand, Rahab was a Canaanite with a sketchy past who only knew about God through hearsay. Yet Rahab and Abraham are considered right with God through their belief and behavior.

Abraham took Isaac, his son, and was willing to sacrifice his life as instructed because he believed in God. Rahab was willing to hide the spies because she believed in God. The faith of neither Rahab nor Abraham showed ritual piety to God's laws and commands. They made a commitment to God through their actions.

Our faith has to be more than an inward belief. It has to be seen in what we do. Our actions have to be more than piety in the way we live. They are to be what looks like reckless abandonment to the mercy and kindness of God.

We have to be willing to obey God in times that are difficult and challenging, and to be willing to test our belief in the faithfulness of God. Our faith in action is when we are willing to step out of our comfort when it is at great cost to ourselves. It is a faith that compels us to do what we believe to be right regardless of whether we will see right done to ourselves. Our faith in action is a willingness to join God in the action of His purposes and plans.

Let's commit to being courageous women of faith like Rahab, who put our faith into action. Let's be women who will risk our lives being obedient to God, to step up when and where we see God at work.

Lord God, I want to be a courageous woman who shows by what I do that I have faith and trust in You. These are the fears I want to let go of (honestly identify and name the pressures, emotions, or anxieties that have kept you from stepping out in faith):

_____

_____

_____

_____ .

Thank You for patiently walking with me as I grow in faith. I want to be brave. I want to show I am committed to You by my actions. I am willing to do what You are calling me to do to fulfill Your purposes. Today, I ask You to show me where You want me to step out for You. (Write down what you sense from God.)

_____

_____ .

Amen.

A WOMAN
WITH MANY ROLES
Deborah

Deborah lived during the period of the judges. The period of time began following the death of Joshua and ended with the establishment of the monarchy.

God raised up individual judges to lead His people and deliver them from their enemies. Deborah was one of those deliverers. At the time of Deborah, the Israelites were oppressed by Jabin king of Canaan.[a]

The time of the judges had a cyclical pattern. When the people forgot God and "did evil in the eyes of the LORD" (Judges 4:1), they experienced the oppression of their enemies. In their misery, they would cry out to God. In His compassion, God would appoint a judge to deliver them from their oppressors. When the judge died, the cycle began all over again.[b]

Deborah, we are going to discover, had many roles. Being in leadership usually doesn't mean just one role, even for us. We can be leaders in our professional spheres, leaders in our church communities, and leaders at home. We are going to learn from Deborah about our many leadership roles and where to focus our attention.

[a] Again the Israelites did evil in the eyes of the LORD . . . So the LORD sold them into the hands of Jabin king of Canaan, who reigned in Hazor. Sisera, the commander of his army, was based in Harosheth Haggoyim (Judges 4:1–2).

[b] Read Judges 2:10–23.

OUR ROLES

Now Deborah, a prophet, the wife of Lappidoth,
was leading Israel at that time.

JUDGES 4:4

Deborah is conspicuous in the Bible as a woman in leadership. In a patriarchal, male-dominated society, Deborah stood out as an extraordinary woman in the positions assigned to her by God.

First and foremost, Deborah was a prophet. Only a few female prophets are named in the Bible; Miriam is one of them (day 53). Chosen by God, prophets served primarily as God's spokespersons.[a] When the prophet gave God's message, it was as if God Himself was speaking.

Deborah had a second significant role as the leader of Israel. When the people cried out to God in their distress, God chose Deborah to govern Israel and to deliver them from the oppressive rule of Jabin, the king of Canaan.

Deborah is noticeable among the other women we have followed so far. Motherhood played a central role in their lives, apart from Miriam. With Deborah, although we know she was married, motherhood is not mentioned. We do not know if Deborah had children. God had other just as significant plans for Deborah. She was to deliver His people at a specific time in history from a specific people.

We can find it difficult when the roles we fill do not fit within the norms of society or are unlike the community around us. Maybe you have a prominent position in government, business, or ministry surrounded by men. Maybe you have enormous responsibility in your role making

[a] I will raise up a prophet like you from among their fellow Israelites. I will put my words in his mouth, and he will tell the people everything I command him (Deuteronomy 18:18 NLT).

life-changing decisions for people or directing the course of society. Or you could stand out in your marital status as a single woman who has never been married. Perhaps out of choice, you do not have children.

Life seems easier when we fit in. Being conspicuous in what we do and how we live can be hard. We often have to explain ourselves. Other people may question our positions or see our roles as inappropriate for women. Maybe you question yourself too. Perhaps you worry if you "have what it takes" to be different or you're just tired of standing out.

Let's pray to receive God's affirmation that—when we genuinely seek God and His ways for us—we are exactly where He wants us to be. Let's pray to have confidence, instead of doubting, the roles God has assigned for us.

Lord God, these are my roles:

_____

_____

_____ .

Sometimes I have doubts about my position, or others doubt my role(s), and that makes me (write down your concerns)

_____

_____

_____ .

As I seek You and Your ways, reassure me that where I am and what I am doing are exactly where You want me to be and what you want me to do. (Talk to God about the reassurance He gives you.)

_____

_____

_____ .

I ask for confidence from You to carry out the tasks You want me to do. Amen.

DAY 67

ATTENTIVE TO GOD

She held court under the Palm of Deborah between Ramah and Bethel
in the hill country of Ephraim, and the Israelites went up to her to have
their disputes decided.

JUDGES 4:5

Deborah "held court" at her place of work known as the "Palm of Deborah" (Judges 4:5). As leader of Israel she had a judicial role, giving advice and judgment to Israel's citizens. Her role sounds similar to that of Moses, who "took his seat to serve as judge for the people, and they stood around him from morning till evening" (Exodus 18:13). We get an understanding of this role when Moses described it as "whenever they have a dispute, it is brought to me, and I decide between the parties and inform them of God's decrees and instructions" (Exodus 18:16).

Deborah established a location for herself where the people could find her—under a tree named after her. Deborah's wisdom and faithfulness to God stood out among the people who, at that time, turned their backs on God. They trusted Deborah to handle their disagreements fairly during a time of trouble and disruption. Deborah was dependable as a woman who listened to God, heard from God, and spoke His words.

As we lead, we not only want to be accessible to those who are our responsibility, but we want to be known as women who are honorable. We should be women who are distinguishable by our honesty and trustworthiness. We want others to perceive us as women who trust in God, listen for His direction, and follow His leading.

Yesterday, you prayed for confidence in the role God has for you. Today, pray to be wise in your role. Practice listening for God's voice instead of what you tell yourself. Establish your role with a foundation of dependence on God so that you can be seen as dependable by those you lead.

Lord God, I want to be a woman who is wise. I want to be a woman who is attentive to Your voice. I commit to listening to You, being dependent on You, and trusting You to lead me.

(Talk to God about specific ways you will commit to listening to Him, whether this is working through these devotions, reading His Word the Bible, spending time with Him in prayer, joining a Bible study, or some other way.) I commit to

_____

_____

_____ .

May the words I speak and the wisdom I give come from listening to You and not myself. Amen.

GIVING ASSURANCE

Barak said to her, "If you go with me, I will go; but if you don't go with me, I won't go." "Certainly I will go with you," said Deborah. "But because of the course you are taking, the honor will not be yours, for the LORD will deliver Sisera into the hands of a woman." So Deborah went with Barak to Kedesh. There Barak summoned Zebulun and Naphtali, and ten thousand men went up under his command. Deborah also went up with him.

JUDGES 4:8–10

Deborah the prophet had a specific command from God for Barak: "The LORD, the God of Israel, commands you: 'Go, take with you ten thousand men of Naphtali and Zebulun and lead them up to Mount Tabor. I will lead Sisera, the commander of Jabin's army, with his chariots and his troops to the Kishon River and give him into your hands'" (Judges 4:6–7).

Barak faced a formidable army of "nine hundred chariots fitted with iron" (Judges 4:3). Yet even with ten thousand men behind him and God as commander-in-chief, Barak feared the army of Sisera more than he feared God's authority and strength over the enemy. Barak did not have the courage to do as God commanded. Barak's hesitation would cost him the glory of personally taking Sisera captive.

Instead, Barak wanted Deborah by his side.

Deborah gave Barak confidence not because she was a military leader, women did not go into battle, but because Barak knew God would give Deborah success. God had given Deborah authority to lead His people. God was with Deborah. Deborah had also placed her confidence in God. With Deborah by his side, Barak would have God with him.

Those we lead can lack faith or have no faith in God. As we lead, we want to instill confidence because we do trust in God and His strength and authority over circumstances. Our faith in God should be the foundation of our leadership. Looking for God's guidance and trusting His direction should be how we lead. Then whatever we face, we can be confident the outcome will be from God.

Pray to stand out in your role because you are a woman whose confidence is placed firmly in God whom you trust as you lead.

Lord God, what I face in my leadership role may look like a formidable foe or a considerable challenge. (Write down one or two challenges you face.)

_____

_____

_____ .

Yet I am reminded my confidence is in You. May my confidence in You be clear to those I lead who lack faith or have no faith. (Read these words from Psalm 71:5–8, then journal about the qualities you can nurture to show your confidence in God.)

"For you have been my hope, Sovereign LORD, my confidence since my youth. From birth I have relied on you; you brought me forth from my mother's womb. I will ever praise you. I have become a sign to many; you are my strong refuge. My mouth is filled with your praise, declaring your splendor all day long."

_____

_____

_____

_____

_____ .

Amen.

THE LORD GOES AHEAD OF YOU

Then Deborah said to Barak, "Go! This is the day the LORD has given Sisera into your hands. Has not the LORD gone ahead of you?" So Barak went down Mount Tabor, with ten thousand men following him.

JUDGES 4:14

Once again, Deborah the prophet spoke God's words and gave Barak the command to "go" and that God had gone ahead of him, securing victory (Judges 4:14). So Barak went.

Deborah had given Barak the confidence to go into battle alone. Barak became the leader he needed to be. Deborah didn't step into the role for him. She did not go into battle and fight. Instead, she enabled Barak to take on his God-given role. It wasn't just Barak whom Deborah encouraged to step out and be courageous, but ten thousand men. Deborah didn't just give Barak confidence; she gave him confidence in God. Barak is commended for a faith that says he "conquered kingdoms" (Hebrews 11:33).[a] Barak, who at first hesitated to trust God and follow His command, grew in his faith in God.

"Has not the LORD gone ahead of you?" (Judges 4:14). These words are a reminder of God's words spoken to Moses and Joshua: "The LORD himself goes before you and will be with you; he will never leave you nor forsake you. Do not be afraid; do not be discouraged" (Deuteronomy 31:8). These are God's words spoken to you too. Whatever

[a] And what more shall I say? I do not have time to tell about Gideon, Barak, Samson and Jephthah, about David and Samuel and the prophets, who through faith conquered kingdoms, administered justice, and gained what was promised; who shut the mouths of lions (Hebrews 11:32–33).

battle you face, whatever difficulty you are working through, God goes before you. We still have to fight, but we can be assured we are not alone.

We can also empower others to believe God's words for themselves. Through our conviction that God is winning our battles, we can give confidence to others so they grow in God-given confidence. When we see people take on the role God has for them, we too will be encouraged. We may even see thousands of people step out in faith.

(Write down how you are trusting God to give you victory in the challenges you wrote about on day 68; be specific.) Lord God, I give You praise because You go before me and You will be with me. I am believing and trusting You will

_____

_____

_____ .

Thank You that I do not need to be afraid of or discouraged by

_____

_____ .

As I lead, may my faith and trust that You are winning my battles empower others to trust in You. Amen.

THE LORD OF HOSTS

At Barak's advance, the LORD routed Sisera and all his chariots and
army by the sword, and Sisera got down from his chariot and fled on
foot. Barak pursued the chariots and army as far as Harosheth Haggoyim, and all Sisera's troops fell by the sword; not a man was left.

JUDGES 4:15–16

God told Barak that He would go ahead of him, and God was true to His
word. God threw Sisera and his army into confusion. God told Barak
that He would give Sisera into his hands, although because of Barak's hesitation, Sisera would be overcome by a woman. Seeing Sisera flee on foot
must have confirmed to Barak that God is true to His word.

The title given to God in this fighting role is Lord of Hosts. *Lord
of Hosts* is a name for God we rarely use nowadays. In this story, the
title conveys God as the commander-in-chief fighting a physical battle
for His people, Israel. God fought for His people against enemies who
exceeded them in power and might, but God was victorious because He
is all-powerful.

God won the battle but not without His people fighting with Him. God
won the battle but not without Deborah's leadership.

The title Lord of Hosts also conveys God as the commander of heavenly
armies who fight spiritual battles. Ephesians 6:12 gives us a clearer idea of
the battles we face: "our struggle is not against flesh and blood, but against
the rulers, against the authorities, against the powers of this dark world
and against the spiritual forces of evil in the heavenly realms."

We fight our spiritual battles in the same way as Deborah and Barak.
We go into battle with faith in God, who is strong and mighty in power,
and by trusting in His Word. We put on the armor God has given us—the
truth of His words, the righteousness with which we are clothed through

our faith in Jesus Christ, the peace of God, and complete faith in Him.[a]

In our roles as leaders, let's remember our battles are not with other people. The battles we face are against spiritual powers of darkness. We fight knowing that God goes before us as commander of His spiritual army. We fight with our faith and trust in God, with our prayers, and with keeping ourselves in God's Word.

Lord of Hosts, thank You for preparing me for the battles I face with the armor You have given me. I put on that armor right now.

I can stand firm because You give me wisdom and discernment. I can have confidence because I am Your child and I am protected through my faith in Jesus Christ. I can be bold because faith in You extinguishes lies, deception, and all that threatens to derail me. I have Your words to follow to make my path straight.

Help me to remember that my conflicts are not with other people but with a spiritual enemy. (Tell God how you will approach your challenges differently knowing they are spiritual battles, and that God fights for you and equips you.)

Amen.

WOMEN WITH SWAY

But Jael, Heber's wife, picked up a tent peg and a hammer and went quietly to him while he lay fast asleep, exhausted. She drove the peg through his temple into the ground, and he died. Just then Barak came by in pursuit of Sisera, and Jael went out to meet him. "Come," she said, "I will show you the man you're looking for." So he went in with her, and there lay Sisera with the tent peg through his temple—dead.

JUDGES 4:21–22

God would "deliver Sisera into the hands of a woman" (Judges 4:9),[a] and sure enough, it happened just as God said. That woman would not be Deborah, the leader of Israel, but Jael, an ordinary housewife.

Imagine Barak's shock when he entered Jael's tent. Imagine the humiliation of Sisera, the commander of the army of nine hundred chariots fitted with iron, had he known he would be killed by a woman.

Battles were fought by men. Yet Israel's battles were fought by God, and He could use anyone He wanted to win those battles, even a woman.

Jael was not a leader; she was a wife who kept house, in this case, a tent. Jael would have been skilled with a hammer and tent peg as, for tent-dwelling people, it was women's work to set up the tent.[b] We don't know what motivated Jael, but her heroic although gruesome act reminds us of Rahab's bravery. Perhaps Jael too knew that

[a] "Certainly I will go with you," said Deborah. "But because of the course you are taking, the honor will not be yours, for the LORD will deliver Sisera into the hands of a woman" (Judges 4:9).

[b] "It was a Kenite woman's responsibility to pitch tents and take them down when it was time to move on, so she would have been swift and accurate in her use of the tent peg."[1]

God was "the LORD your God [who] is God in heaven above and on the earth below" (Joshua 2:11).

Jael swayed the outcome of the battle. Deborah calls her blessed and praised her action: "Most blessed of women be Jael, the wife of Heber the Kenite, most blessed of tent-dwelling women. He asked for water, and she gave him milk; in a bowl fit for nobles she brought him curdled milk. Her hand reached for the tent peg, her right hand for the workman's hammer. She struck Sisera, she crushed his head, she shattered and pierced his temple. At her feet he sank, he fell; there he lay. At her feet he sank, he fell; where he sank, there he fell—dead" (Judges 5:24–27).

Jael might not have had a formal leadership role in the battle, but Deborah recognized that God empowered Jael to rise up and secure the Israelites' victory.

As women, let's not underestimate the good things God can do through us and other women—although hopefully not in such a grisly way. Let's pray that we may encourage women, whatever their roles, to know that God can use them for His purposes.

Lord God, thank You that whatever my role or position at work or home, You can use me for Your purposes in any and every way You want. I make myself available to You with the skills of

_____

_____ .

Show me how I can encourage and empower other women to know they are valuable to You and Your purposes. (Write down names of women God brings to mind to encourage and empower.)

_____

_____

_____ .

Never let me underestimate the way You work through women. Amen.

LEADING OTHERS TO PRAISE GOD

On that day Deborah and Barak son of Abinoam sang this song:
"When the princes in Israel take the lead, when the people willingly
offer themselves—praise the LORD!"

JUDGES 5:1–2

Deborah the prophet and leader of Israel stepped into another leadership role once the battle was won. Deborah became a songwriter and worship leader.

Deborah and Barak wrote the song not just to be sung in the euphoria of victory but as a reminder for years to come, even today, that God fights for His people and frees them from oppression when they cry out to Him.

Deborah and Barak's praise acknowledged that when people were willing to trust God, when they were willing to step up in leadership, God acted on their behalf.

The generation of Deborah had turned away from God and forgotten what He had done for them in the past. Deborah reminded them through song that when the God of Israel marched into battle on behalf of His people, "the earth shook, the heavens poured, the clouds poured down water. The mountains quaked before the LORD" (Judges 5:4–5).

God raised up judges like Deborah to bring His people back to Him. Deborah's job was to encourage the people that they were to renew their trust in God who had chosen them as His people. When they wholeheartedly trusted God, He fought for them.

You might not be a songwriter or a worship leader, but in any role, you can bring praise to God by helping others recognize the goodness of God. You can remind them of what God has done in their lives, the battles He has won in the past. You can encourage them to trust God wholeheartedly by talking about your own faith in God and the battles He has won for you. You can point out that God is just as faithful today as He has been in the past.

Whatever role you are in, whether it is at work or at home, pray about the opportunities to lead others to praise God.

Lord God, I give You praise. I praise You for Your goodness to me and the battles You have won for me:

_____

_____

_____ .

As I lead, whether at work or at home, let me never forget to give praise to You where it is due. May I speak of the victories You have given me and remind others of the battles You can win for them when they trust in You. Amen.

(Think about how you can express to someone who doesn't know God, or who does not have the same faith as you, what God has done for you in overcoming one of the challenges you wrote above.)

_____

_____

_____

_____ .

A MOTHER IN LEADERSHIP

Villagers in Israel would not fight; they held back until I, Deborah, arose, until I arose, a mother in Israel.

JUDGES 5:7

Deborah had yet another role, that of mother to Israel. This role she assigned to herself. From this designation, we learn the heart of her leadership—her deep love for the Israelites as if they were her own children.

At a time when "the highways were abandoned" and "travelers took to winding paths" (Judges 5:6) because the people lived in fear and dread of their oppressor, Deborah arose like a mother coming to rescue her children. When "not a shield or spear was seen among forty thousand in Israel" (Judges 5:8), Deborah as a mother encouraged them to have the courage and will to fight against the Canaanites. When "Israel's princes, with the willing volunteers among the people" (Judges 5:9) showed the courage to fight, Deborah—like an overprotective mother—demonstrated the highest concern for their welfare. Just as a mother has admiration for the successes of her children, Deborah took pride in their victories: "Consider the voice of the singers at the watering places. They recite the victories of the LORD, the victories of his villagers in Israel" (Judges 5:10–11). Deborah celebrated her motherly role.

Leadership, Deborah teaches us, does not have to be cold and dispassionate. It can be nurturing, caring, loving, protective, and encouraging. Motherly instincts used in leadership are valued elsewhere in the Bible. The apostle Paul saw himself as loving and caring for the Christians in Thessalonica like a nursing mother cossets her child: "Just as a nursing mother cares for her children, so we cared for you" (1 Thessalonians 2:7–8). Jesus speaks of Himself as like a protective mother hen: "How often I have longed to gather your children together, as a hen gathers her chicks under her wings" (Luke 13:34).

Be encouraged that you can use characteristics that come instinctively to you as a woman in your leadership roles. You might enjoy encouraging the development of those you lead. You might believe it is important to protectively watch over those you look after. You might lead from a supporting role, always available to give help. Let's be women who embrace our motherly instincts as we lead.

Lord God, these are the instincts that come naturally to me:

_____

_____

_____ .

Give me wisdom to know when and how I can use these instincts in my leadership roles.

(Spend a few moments telling God the areas in your life where you can make the most of these natural abilities.)

_____

_____

_____ .

Amen.

CELEBRATING

Then the people of the LORD went down to the city gates. "Wake up, wake up, Deborah! Wake up, wake up, break out in song! Arise, Barak! Take captive your captives, son of Abinoam."

JUDGES 5:11–12

The song celebrates the people who came to Deborah to awaken her into action, to deliver them from the oppression of Jabin king of Canaan. God had raised up Deborah as a deliverer for Israel. God had given her the role of prophet, judge, and deliverer to muster the people to fight.

Some tribes in Israel responded positively to Deborah's call to action: "The remnant of the nobles came down; the people of the LORD came down to me against the mighty. Some came from Ephraim, whose roots were in Amalek; Benjamin was with the people who followed you. From Makir captains came down, from Zebulun those who bear a commander's staff. The princes of Issachar were with Deborah; yes, Issachar was with Barak, sent under his command into the valley. . . . The people of Zebulun risked their very lives; so did Naphtali on the terraced fields" (Judges 5:13–15, 18).

Others did not: "In the districts of Reuben there was much searching of heart. Why did you stay among the sheep pens to hear the whistling for the flocks? In the districts of Reuben there was much searching of heart. Gilead stayed beyond the Jordan. And Dan, why did he linger by the ships? Asher remained on the coast and stayed in his coves" (4:15–17). These people were either complacent or preoccupied with their lives; they didn't see the battle as important.

Deborah, however, was not afraid to celebrate in song with those who did join her because God was fighting with them: "From the heavens the stars fought, from their courses they fought against Sisera" (5:20). They reversed the oppression of the last twenty years.

As God calls us into roles of leadership, particularly those for His purposes, not everyone will share in our vision, want to join us, or see the importance of the task. They may even oppose our choice of direction. When we encounter these reactions, we should not see them as a reflection of our leadership. No matter what path is clearly from God, not everyone will feel the same way as you.

Let's celebrate where God has us and what He is doing. Let's keep our eyes focused on God's leading and guidance. Let's be excited to be used for His plans and purposes.

Lord God, thank You for the roles You have given me of

_____

_____ .

I celebrate all that I have been able to do so far:

_____

_____ .

I celebrate all that I hope to do in the future:

_____

_____ .

Amen.

A UNIQUE UNDERSTANDING

Through the window peered Sisera's mother; behind the lattice she cried out, "Why is his chariot so long in coming? Why is the clatter of his chariots delayed?" The wisest of her ladies answer her; indeed, she keeps saying to herself, "Are they not finding and dividing the spoils: a woman or two for each man, colorful garments as plunder for Sisera, colorful garments embroidered, highly embroidered garments for my neck—all this as plunder?"

JUDGES 5:28–30

Deborah gives a unique view of battle seen from the perspective of women. Deborah introduced us to Jael, already mentioned on day 71, whose brave but gruesome act of killing Sisera clinched the battle for the Israelites. Deborah also considered the battle from the viewpoint of Sisera's mother. Sisera's mother questioned why her son, usually victorious in his military endeavors, was taking so long to return home. Love for her son kept her at the window waiting to catch a glimpse of him. Her female attendants, in attempting to reassure Sisera's mother, seem indifferent to the effects of war on other women—"a woman or two for each man" (Judges 5:30). These words describe the rape of women and girls as an outcome of victory.

The realities of war for women in this song are sadly the realities we still face today. Women can be heroes in battle, bereaved from lost loved ones, and victims who are subject to sexual violence in war and as a deliberate tactic of warfare.

You may have been personally affected by war or other tragic circumstances, and as a woman, you too have a unique perspective on the circumstances of war for yourself or other women and girls, whether at home or across the world.

Whatever situation we find ourselves in, as leaders or as observers, let's be cognizant like Deborah to the plights of other women, to their joys and their sadnesses, to their victories and their defeats, to whatever they experience.

As women, whatever our roles, let's pray for wisdom to use the influence we have to be observant of the struggles of other women, and the extent of their plights. Let's also be women who are willing to step up and take action, to see where God, who cares for the plight of women, would want us to join Him in His work. Pray for God to awaken you to what you can do.

Lord God, many women are suffering at home and across the world (write down suffering that you notice):

_____

_____

_____

Show me where You want me to step up and do my part for the plight of women. Awaken me to be a compassionate leader for Your good purposes. Amen.

(Write down where God is prompting you to act in both small and bigger ways.)

_____

_____

_____

_____

A WOMAN OF TRAGEDY
Naomi

Naomi lived "in the days when the judges ruled" (Ruth 1:1). During this period of time, as we learned from Deborah, "the Israelites did evil in the eyes of the LORD" (Judges 2:11). However, the book of Ruth zooms in on the story of two women, one who is Naomi, and the community of Bethlehem that remained loyal to God.

Naomi lived in Bethlehem with her husband and two sons. They relocated to Moab, roughly thirty miles away from Bethlehem on the southeastern side of the Dead Sea to wait out the famine in the land of Judah. Moving to avoid a famine was not uncommon. Abraham and Sarah did something similar when they moved to Egypt.[a]

Naomi suffered great personal tragedy in her life, yet God in His kindness provided for all her needs. We will learn that even in our own tragedies, God is kind. He is a God who provides for all our needs too. Through God's kindness, we can know fulfillment even when we experience emptiness in our lives.

[a] Now there was a famine in the land, and Abram went down to Egypt to live there for a while because the famine was severe (Genesis 12:10).

FACING TRAGEDY

Now Elimelek, Naomi's husband, died, and she was left with her two sons. They married Moabite women, one named Orpah and the other Ruth. After they had lived there about ten years, both Mahlon and Kilion also died, and Naomi was left without her two sons and her husband.

RUTH 1:3–5

Naomi's world had been turned upside down. She and her family relocated to Moab, leaving all that they knew, to escape the famine, then disaster struck. First her husband died and then both her sons. Naomi's life went from plenty to empty. Naomi suddenly found herself alone in a foreign land away from friends, family, and her family of faith.

The three most important people in her life were gone, but so was her support system. She had no husband or sons to provide for her or the future. Naomi faced instant poverty and a future of destitution, as women were unable to inherit land or wealth from their husbands.

Alongside the grief and poverty, Naomi suffered the disgrace of not providing an heir to continue the family line. She faced disapproval and criticism even though the loss of her husband and sons was beyond her control.

God, however, has a special love and concern for widows.

Losing a loved one is one of life's most stressful and emotionally challenging experiences. We can feel a range of emotions, from intense despair to shock and even guilt. Losing a partner can also lead to deep financial concerns for the present as well as the future.

Experiencing tragedy is not limited to the loss of a loved one. A debilitating accident, a divorce, being a victim of crime, even relocating to another country can mean deep grief and anguish. These types of losses leave us feeling that we too have gone from a life of plenty to one that is empty.

Just as God is especially attentive to the plight of widows, He has a special concern for us when we experience heartache and pain, whatever our circumstances. One day God will wipe away all our tears and there will be "'no more death' or mourning or crying or pain" (Revelation 21:4).

As we begin Naomi's story, take time to think about your own story of tragedy. Write out your story of suffering.

Lord God, this is my story of suffering (write down the facts, the events, and details):

_____

_____

_____

_____

_____

_____

_____

_____

_____

_____

_____

_____

_____

_____

Amen.

FINDING GOD'S PROVISION

When Naomi heard in Moab that the LORD had come to the aid of
his people by providing food for them, she and her daughters-in-law
prepared to return home from there. With her two daughters-in-law
she left the place where she had been living and set out on the road
that would take them back to the land of Judah.

RUTH 1:6–7

A mid the darkness that settled on her life, Naomi heard good news that
brought a glimmer of hope into her world. Back home in Bethlehem,
the famine was over. Her people had food.

God had "come to the aid of his people" (Ruth 1:6). God was on the
move to provide for His people. Even in the times of the judges when people
were "evil in the eyes of the LORD" (Judges 2:11). *Providence* is the word
to describe God guiding and governing events and circumstances for the
needs of His people. God had not forgotten or abandoned His people. God
in His grace had provided rain to bring a harvest.

Naomi wanted to be a recipient of God's provision too. So Naomi left
Moab. She began the journey back to Bethlehem from across the other side
of the Jordan River. She wanted to be in the place where God was at work.

We want to be recipients of God's provision and kindness too. God, the
Bible tells us, is kind to everyone: "He has shown kindness by giving you
rain from heaven and crops in their seasons; he provides you with plenty of
food and fills your hearts with joy" (Acts 14:17), and "The LORD is good
to everyone. He showers compassion on all his creation" (Psalm 145:9
NLT). God's kindness extends to you.

We also want to be recipients of God's specific provision and kindness
when we are struggling in our personal circumstances. Like Naomi, we should
go to be where God is present among His people. In the wider community
of God's people, we can find encouragement and support, and a focus on

God's goodness that we are unable to find on our own. In times of empti-ness, we need a community that is full of God's love, grace, and goodness.

If you are in the middle of deep tragedy, the darkness of grief, ask God for a glimmer of hope. Even in our small daily struggles, we are invited to look for glimpses of God at work extending His kindness to us.

Lord God, thank You that You shower Your kindness on all creation. You are kind by (write down ways you see God's kindness in the natural world)

_____

_____ .

As I look for glimpses of Your compassion in everyday ways, I see You provide for me by

_____

_____

_____ .

Let me see You at work, showing me Your kindness and giving me glim-mers of hope through Your provision and/or people to encourage and support me. (Write down specific resources and people that have helped you.) Thank You for

_____

_____

_____ .

Amen.

WHEN KINDNESS IS NEAR

Then Naomi said to her two daughters-in-law, "Go
back, each of you, to your mother's home. May the
LORD show you kindness, as you have shown kindness
to your dead husbands and to me. May the LORD
grant that each of you will find rest in the home of
another husband."

RUTH 1:8–9

Naomi realized, as she and her two daughters-in-law
trudged along the road to Bethlehem, that kindness
had been close by after all. Orpah and Ruth had been
kind to her.

These two widows had stayed with Naomi after the
death of their husbands. They had been good companions.
They had provided company in her loneliness and comfort
to her as they shared in their grief.

Naomi felt it unkind to expect Orpah and Ruth to stay
with her. Although bonded in their experiences, Naomi
summoned up the courage to release these two women
from their duty to her. By urging them to return home,
she freed them of the responsibility they felt toward her.

Naomi repeated the instruction to "return home."[a]
Orpah and Ruth had a better chance of finding husbands
from among their families in Moab than as foreigners in
Bethlehem. Naomi had no more sons who could be their
husbands. The most considerate direction and guidance

[a] Read Ruth
1:11–13.

Naomi could give to her daughters-in-law was to persuade them to *return home*, even though it meant going on to Bethlehem alone.

Forefront in Naomi's mind was asking God to show His kindness to these women, and that was Naomi's prayer for them. Naomi knew the truth about this attribute of God. God's generosity isn't just for His people; God's benevolence is for all people, even women from Moab who worshiped foreign gods rather than the one true God.

Kindness is an important concept in our lives too, both knowing the kindness of God and receiving and showing kindness to other people. We can experience the love and empathy of other women who share the same challenges, grief, and stresses we do, even if they are not of the same faith. These women can be just who we need when no one else understands.

We may find it hard to reciprocate kindness in the depths of grief, but we can pray for God to show His goodness to those who help us. Let's be women who, like Naomi, are kind in all circumstances. Pray for other women to know God's kindness in their lives. Pray for God to shower them with His love, goodness, and mercy because God is good and kind to all.

Lord God, You are kind, gracious, and compassionate to everyone. I ask for You to show Your kindness to (list friends, acquaintances, and loved ones you'd like to intercede for)

_____

_____

_____

Lavish each woman with Your love, goodness, and grace. Grant each of them (write down each name again and, by it, one specific kindness or generosity you would like God to show to each woman)

_____

_____

_____

Amen.

FEELING BITTER

No, my daughters. It is more bitter for me than for you, because the LORD's hand has turned against me!

RUTH 1:13

Although Orpah and Ruth share the same loss and hardship of widowhood, Naomi's distress was worse because God had turned against *her*. We have been aware of Naomi's mental anguish from her tragic circumstances. But in a final outburst to Orpah and Ruth, we learn of her spiritual suffering.

Naomi knew that God was kind. She understood He could be gracious to her foreign daughters-in-law who followed foreign gods. She had prayed God would show goodness to them. She knew God had shown mercy to His people back in Bethlehem. God's kindness, however, did not extend to her.

"The Lord's hand," found in Ruth 1:13, is a term used to describe God coming in His power.[a] In Naomi's lifetime, in the time of the judges, *the Lord's hand* often came against His people to defeat them in battle because they had forsaken the Lord and done "evil in the eyes of the Lord."[b]

Just as God had displayed His anger against the nation and brought them great distress, it seems Naomi thought God had done the same to her.

Tragedy can lead us to question God's kindness toward us. A life-threatening diagnosis, the death of someone we love dearly, or a debilitating accident can make us consider if we have done something wrong to deserve what has happened to us. We may think we have displeased God, that

[a] "The hand of God is the symbol of his power."[1]

[b] Read Judges 2:10–15.

the disaster is punishment. We can feel that God has turned His back on us. It's natural to struggle to understand what has happened to us.

As women of faith, we should not feel ashamed of our thoughts about God. Nor should we be hesitant to bring our feelings to God. Even Jesus prayed: "My God, my God, why have you forsaken me?" (Matthew 27:46; Mark 15:34).

Let's be women who pray honestly to God about the way we are feeling.

Lord God, I have shared with You the facts about my story of suffering (recap what you wrote in your prayer on day 76):

_____

_____

_____ .

Now I am being honest with You about how I feel. I am

_____

_____ .

I feel like You

_____

_____ .

I also ask, *why*

_____

_____ ?

Amen.

EXPRESSING BITTERNESS

So the two women went on until they came to Beth-lehem. When they arrived in Bethlehem, the whole town was stirred because of them, and the women exclaimed, "Can this be Naomi?" "Don't call me Naomi," she told them. "Call me Mara, because the Almighty has made my life very bitter. I went away full, but the Lord has brought me back empty. Why call me Naomi? The Lord has afflicted me; the Almighty has brought misfortune upon me."

RUTH 1:19–21

News spread like wildfire in Bethlehem as Naomi walked into town. And Naomi immediately had an audience. All the women came to see her.

I would imagine that Naomi, whose name means "pleas-ant" or "sweet,"[a] had left for Moab with such confidence of a satisfying life. Food on the table, sons to be married, grandchildren to look forward to.

The women of Bethlehem barely recognized her as the same person when she turned up in town. Grief and anxiety can change us. It can affect our physical appearance and cause us to age prematurely.

Ruth 1:18 says, "The whole town was *stirred* because of them" (emphasis added). The Hebrew word for *stirred* means "to confuse." Maybe the women of the town were baffled by Naomi's appearance and outburst that "the

[a] "Naomi (Nā ō' mĭ): Personal name meaning 'my pleasantness.'"[2]

LORD has afflicted me" (1:21). Maybe they didn't understand her bitterness toward God because they have never suffered tragedy.

Maybe you can tell that others are shocked by your appearance. Maybe you don't stand as upright as you used to. You notice the new lines and the extra gray hairs as you look in the mirror. You now tighten the belt on the pants that used to threaten to burst a button.

Our grief and anxiety can mean we cause a stir in our family or church family. Other people's reactions can be a mixture of puzzled, troubled, shaken up, or stunned.

Not everyone will understand our emotional or spiritual struggle. We should choose carefully with whom we share. Those who do understand what we are going through will not be put off by our outbursts. Naomi had made the same accusations about God to Ruth as she did to the women of Bethlehem, and yet Ruth had chosen "your God [is] my God" (1:16).

As we continue with the story of Naomi, we will see that her bitterness does not deter God's kindness toward her. It is the same for you.

Pray for people to come into your life who understand your emotional and spiritual struggles.

Lord God, I will remember that, especially when I am struggling and weak, You draw near to me and demonstrate Your exceeding kindness and love. Thank You for never leaving me or abandoning me and for being present in my distress. I sit for a moment with You and ask You to reveal Your tenderheartedness to me.

(Read the following words from God and repeat back to God in your own words what you hear from Him.)

"The LORD is close to the brokenhearted and saves those who are crushed in spirit" (Psalm 34:18). Lord,

———————————————————————————————— .

"When you go through deep waters, I will be with you. When you go through rivers of difficulty, you will not drown. When you walk through the fire of oppression, you will not be burned up; the flames will not consume you" (Isaiah 43:2 NLT). Lord,

_____

_____ .

I ask You to bring people into my life who understand my struggles. I ask You to give me friends in whom I can confide, who will stand by my side no matter what. (As God answers your prayer, write down the names of those people He brings to mind.)

_____

_____ .

Thank You for being my faithful, true Friend. Amen.

A GLIMMER OF GOD'S KINDNESS

So Naomi returned from Moab accompanied by
Ruth the Moabite, her daughter-in-law, arriving
in Bethlehem as the barley harvest was beginning.

RUTH 1:22

Ripened barley swayed in the breeze as Naomi and Ruth walked into town. No longer did Naomi see the cracked, dry land that had been the reason for her and her family leaving for Moab. The famine was over. Soon grain would be threshed. Naomi's and Ruth's most basic needs of filling their stomachs would be met. Maybe with the harvest, Naomi saw an opportunity for daily bread and a glimmer of God's kindness toward her. God in His goodness had sent rain from heaven for the crops to grow.[a] Naomi also had been shown kindness by another human being. She had Ruth with her. Naomi was not alone.

God's nature is to be kind, to provide the most basic needs for all humanity and all his creatures. Psalm 104:14 describes God's generosity in this way: "He makes grass grow for the cattle, and plants for people to cultivate—bringing forth food from the earth." God's goodness and grace extend to everyone, no matter how people feel about Him,[b] including Naomi in her bitterness toward God.

No matter how much anger or disappointment you feel about your lot in life, find comfort in knowing God's kindness extends to your essential needs. Jesus taught us to pray for our most basic needs: "Give us today our daily

[a] He has shown kindness by giving you rain from heaven and crops in their seasons; he provides you with plenty of food and fills your hearts with joy (Acts 14:17).

[b] For he gives his sunlight to both the evil and the good, and he sends rain on the just and the unjust alike (Matthew 5:45 NLT).

210

bread" (Matthew 6:11). What is essential doesn't have to be food. It can be a sunny morning that makes you eager to get out of bed or the beauty of flowers that brighten your spirits. Even the smallest things we take for granted are provided by God in His kindness.

In His goodness God also provides for more than our basic needs. Philippians 4:19 tells us that "God will meet *all* your needs according to the riches of his glory in Christ Jesus" (emphasis added).

Use this prayer, paraphrased from the Lord's Prayer found in Matthew 6:9–13 to ask God in His kindness to meet all that is important to you.

My Father in heaven, You are holy. I honor Your name. I praise You today because

May Your will be done on earth as it is in heaven. May Your will be done in this situation:

Meet my daily needs today of

Meet *all* my needs of

Forgive me for the wrong I have done as I forgive others. Keep me from temptation and evil. In Jesus's name. Amen.

SEEING A TURNAROUND

Then Ruth told her mother-in-law about the one at whose place she had been working. "The name of the man I worked with today is Boaz," she said. "The LORD bless him!" Naomi said to her daughter-in-law. "He has not stopped showing his kindness to the living and the dead." She added, "That man is our close relative; he is one of our guardian-redeemers."

RUTH 2:19–20

[a] When you are harvesting in your field and you overlook a sheaf, do not go back to get it. Leave it for the foreigner, the fatherless and the widow (Deuteronomy 24:19).

[b] [God] defends the cause of the fatherless and the widow, and loves the foreigner residing among you, giving them food and clothing (Deuteronomy 10:18).

If, up to this point, Naomi had struggled to recognize God's specific kindness in her life, Ruth's encounter with Boaz may have changed her mind. Ruth choosing to glean in the fields of Boaz was no coincidence. God had been guiding and presiding over the events that day.

Gleaning was a stipulation in God's law that allowed for people to show kindness to the poor, widows, and foreigners.[a] Gleaning was also a practical way in which God showed His love to those who were downtrodden.[b]

Boaz went above and beyond by allowing Ruth to gather a few stalks of barley for her and Naomi to make bread. Ruth returned home with a leftover meal for Naomi and an ephah, equivalent to thirty to fifty pounds in weight of grain.[3] Boaz was a generous, God-fearing man. Perhaps he learned about kindness from his mother, Rahab, a foreigner who showed great kindness to the spies (day 62).

As we see in this beautiful story about God's kindness and providence, God governs and oversees all the activities of our lives for our good and for His good purposes. And God can use other people to show us His goodness. When a person is able to help us begin to turn around our lives in some small but practical way, let's see it as God's kindness. Let's thank God for that person and ask God to show them kindness in return. When you see even the smallest improvement in any difficult situation, recognize it as God's grace and goodness shown to you. How is God providing for you through the kindness of a friend or family member?

Lord God, thank You for the kindness of (name a coworker, friend, acquaintance, or loved one)

_____ .

Thank You for Your goodness shown in (write down the way in which the person just mentioned provided for you)

_____

_____ .

I ask You to show Your kindness, compassion, and grace to this person by providing him/her with

_____

_____

in bigger and better ways than I could even ask. Amen.

A GUARDIAN-REDEEMER

So Boaz took Ruth and she became his wife. When he made love to her, the LORD enabled her to conceive, and she gave birth to a son. The women said to Naomi: "Praise be to the LORD, who this day has not left you without a guardian-redeemer. May he become famous throughout Israel! He will renew your life and sustain you in your old age. For your daughter-in-law, who loves you and who is better to you than seven sons, has given him birth."

RUTH 4:13–15

Naomi's prayer for God to show kindness to Ruth in providing another husband was indeed answered, but not in the way Naomi expected.[a] Naomi had prayed for a Moabite husband. God had provided a godly Israelite husband who was also Naomi's guardian-redeemer.

Guardian-redeemers were another of God's provisions for family members who encountered trouble and poverty. Guardian-redeemers could purchase land on behalf of relatives who were in financial difficulty, thereby freeing them from poverty.[b] In Naomi's case, Boaz, as her guardian-redeemer, purchased the land that belonged to Naomi's husband, Elimelek. Guardian-redeemers could also marry the widow of a relative, freeing her from destitution and enabling the dead man's name to be continued.[c] In taking Ruth as his wife, Boaz provided Naomi with a grandchild to continue the family lineage.

[a] [Naomi said,] "May the LORD show you kindness, as you have shown kindness to your dead husbands and to me. May the LORD grant that each of you will find rest in the home of another husband" (Ruth 1:8–9).

[b] If one of your fellow Israelites becomes poor and sells some of their property, their nearest relative is to come and redeem what they have sold (Leviticus 25:25).

[c] Read Deuteronomy 25:5–6.

God in His kindness and grace has provided for our future too. Jesus is spoken of as a redeemer. He paid the price of His life so that we might have life. That price is called a "ransom." "For even the Son of Man did not come to be served, but to serve, and to give his life as a ransom for many" (Mark 10:45). A ransom is a payment made to release a prisoner. Jesus paid so we might be free from death and sin.

God's hand had never been against Naomi. All along He had been working out His provision for her old age. Naomi's life was filled with tragedy, but God had been with her, providing for her in small ways and lasting ways.

When we are tempted to look at our lot and think that God is against us, we can remember that in His goodness and grace, God provides for us in the day-to-day and for our future, through other people and through His Son.

Naomi was never called *Mara*. Her life did not remain bitter. God in His kindness filled her empty life so it was indeed pleasant.

Lord God, thank You that in the middle of all my troubles Your kindness and grace provide for my day-to-day needs and my future needs. Thank You for Jesus, my Redeemer, who has paid the price for my wrongdoing so I might have life with You. I have shared with You my story of suffering; now I praise You by recounting my story of salvation. (Write down how you came to know Jesus.)

———————————————————————————————————

———————————————————————————————————

———————————————————————————————————

I thank You because I feel (write about the joy, sweetness, and pleasure of knowing Jesus)

———————————————————————————————————

———————————————————————————————————

Amen.

A WOMAN UNDER GOD'S WINGS
Ruth

R uth was a Moabite. Moabites worshiped idols, particularly a god called "Chemosh." Israel regularly abandoned the living Lord God to worship idols, including the gods of Moab.[a] God used Moab to punish his people for their idolatry.[b]

Ruth was also a widow. Naomi's son, Mahlon, had married Ruth in Moab, where the family had fled to avoid the famine in the land of Judah. When Naomi's husband and two sons died leaving Naomi, Ruth, and Orpah as widows, the three women set out toward Bethlehem. On the journey, Naomi urged her daughters-in-law to return to Moab. We join the story with Ruth's response. From Ruth we learn about both human kindness and God's kindness, that no one is excluded from being accepted into His family, whatever their background.

[a] Again the Israelites did evil in the eyes of the LORD. They served the Baals and the Ashtoreths, and the gods of Aram, the gods of Sidon, the gods of Moab, the gods of the Ammonites and the gods of the Philistines (Judges 10:6).

[b] Again the Israelites did evil in the eyes of the LORD, and because they did this evil the LORD gave Eglon king of Moab power over Israel (Judges 3:12).

COMMITMENT

Then Orpah kissed her mother-in-law goodbye, but Ruth clung to her. "Look," said Naomi, "your sister-in-law is going back to her people and her gods. Go back with her." But Ruth replied, "Don't urge me to leave you or to turn back from you. Where you go I will go, and where you stay I will stay. Your people will be my people and your God my God. Where you die I will die, and there I will be buried. May the LORD deal with me, be it ever so severely, if even death separates you and me."

RUTH 1:14–17

Ruth made a complete commitment to Naomi and, as a result of that wholehearted decision, came under the protective care of Naomi's God. Ruth 1:14 says that "Ruth clung" to Naomi.

Clung is the same word used in Genesis 2:24 to describe a commitment in marriage. Ruth's devotion to Naomi was as solemn as marriage vows, "til death do us part." The first words spoken by Ruth confirmed her absolute loyalty to Naomi.

Going home to Moab gave Ruth a greater possibility and probability of finding another husband, the familiarity of her culture, people, and gods, and the security of being surrounded by family.

Ruth, however, was willing to abandon all she knew to step into an unknown and uncertain future. Naomi had already told Ruth there was no hope of her providing another husband.

As an extension of her commitment to Naomi, Ruth was willing to go *all in* with the God of Israel. Ruth was ready to take a risk with God whom Naomi said had "turned against me" (Ruth 1:13). Ruth, however, was undeterred.

At a time in history when God's people were turning away from God, out of devotion to her mother-in-law, a foreign woman from a pagan country placed herself under God's protection.

Ruth's devotion to Naomi is remarkable. Her example of being prepared to trust God can encourage us to do the same. We should aim to emulate her devotion.

Following God can mean being willing to let go of that which is comfortable and predictable in our lives. To follow God's way, we may leave behind a way of life that is all we have ever known. It may mean deciding that God is trustworthy when other people don't believe in the truth of His words. Saying yes to God, whatever stage of our faith journey, can mean stepping out into the unknown.

Use the following prayer to tell God about your willingness, or unwillingness, to *cleave* to Him.

Lord God, as I think about stepping out and going *all in* with You. I realize (tell God what it means to you to go all in with Him)

_____

_____

_____

_____

I am believing that my devotion to You brings me under Your protective care. Amen.

GOD'S PROVISION

And Ruth the Moabite said to Naomi, "Let me go
to the fields and pick up the leftover grain behind
anyone in whose eyes I find favor." Naomi said to her,
"Go ahead, my daughter." So she went out, entered
a field and began to glean behind the harvesters. As
it turned out, she was working in a field belonging
to Boaz, who was from the clan of Elimelek.

RUTH 2:2–3

R uth followed through on her commitment to Naomi.
She traveled with Naomi to Bethlehem, and there they
settled into lives as widows.

Ruth took responsibility to provide food for herself and
Naomi. She went to glean in the fields, to "pick up the
leftover grain behind anyone in whose eyes I find favor"
(Ruth 2:2). We cannot miss that Ruth happened to choose
fields, unknowingly, that belonged "to Boaz, who was from
the clan of Elimelek" (v. 3), a relative of Naomi's husband.

There are no coincidences with God. God had begun to
provide for these two women. We are invited to consider
that God had led Ruth, under His protective care, to the
fields of Boaz, a generous man who followed God's laws.

Boaz put Ruth at ease with his kindness even though
Ruth, as a foreigner, did not even have the status of one
of his servants.[a] Ruth was welcomed as if she were one
of his family, allowing her to eat meals with him and his
workers.[b] Boaz even generously provided for Ruth: "As
she got up to glean, Boaz gave orders to his men, 'Let her
gather among the sheaves and don't reprimand her. Even

[a] Read Ruth 2:13.

[b] At mealtime
Boaz said to her,
"Come over here.
Have some bread
and dip it in the
wine vinegar."
When she sat
down with the
harvesters, he of-
fered her some
roasted grain. She
ate all she wanted
and had some left
over (Ruth 2:14).

pull out some stalks for her from the bundles and leave them for her to pick up, and don't rebuke her'" (2:15–16).

Boaz gives us a picture of God's protective care for us. When we make a commitment to God, He welcomes us into His family even though we may feel like outsiders. He gives us the status of daughter, and child of God.

The generosity of Boaz reminds us of the generosity of God. We can expect His provision to exceed our expectations. Psalm 34:10 (NLT) says, "Those who trust in the LORD will lack no good thing." We will have all we need. God is true to His word. He will provide for you. Thank God for what He has provided and ask Him to meet your needs today.

Lord God, I thank You that trusting in You means You lead me, provide for me, and I lack no good thing. Thank You for Your generosity by providing (write down good things that have happened to you recently)

_____

_____

_____ .

I ask you to meet my need today for

_____

_____ .

Amen.

GOD'S FAVOR

Boaz said to Ruth, "My daughter, listen to me. Don't go and glean in another field and don't go away from here. Stay here with the women who work for me." . . . At this, she bowed down with her face to the ground. She asked him, "Why have I found such favor in your eyes that you notice me—a foreigner?"

RUTH 2:8, 10

It wasn't just the kindness and generosity of Boaz that brought Ruth to her knees. She bowed in astonishment because Ruth—as a foreigner—considered herself an unlikely recipient of his favor.

Boaz was a man who followed God's laws. God had instructed His people that "when a foreigner resides among you in your land, do not mistreat them. The foreigner residing among you must be treated as your native-born. Love them as yourself, for you were foreigners in Egypt" (Leviticus 19:33–34).

It was because Ruth was a foreigner that Boaz had instructed his men to not abuse her.[a] It was because Ruth was a foreigner that he called her "daughter" and treated her like one of his own workers (Ruth 2:8). Boaz welcomed Ruth like a member of his family.

God doesn't welcome just women from Moab into His family. His concern is for all of us who feel like foreigners and outsiders.

God instructed His people to be kind to foreigners because they once were the same. We have to remember that every person in God's family was once outside God's

[a] [Boaz said,] "Watch the field where the men are harvesting, and follow along after the women. I have told the men not to lay a hand on you. And whenever you are thirsty, go and get a drink from the water jars the men have filled" (Ruth 2:9).

family. No one, from the time of Adam and Eve to today, is born into God's family without faith: "For you are all children of God through faith in Christ Jesus" (Galatians 3:26 NLT).

We can feel like we're not accepted into the family of God because our theological beliefs and practices differ from what appears to be the norm. We can believe that our background or past excludes us from God's family. We can think that because we don't do or say the right things, don't pray in the right way, or don't know our way around the Bible that we are on the edges of God's family. However, it is our heartfelt commitment to God that makes us welcome in and part of His family.

When you make a commitment to God, your status changes from foreigner to family. Welcome to being a daughter of God.

(Choose one or more of these verses to thank and praise God for His goodness and mercy to you as revealed in the verses below.)

"See what great love the Father has lavished on us, that we should be called children of God! And that is what we are! The reason the world does not know us is that it did not know him" (1 John 3:1). Heavenly Father, I thank You for

———————————————————————————————————— .

"Therefore, if anyone is in Christ, the new creation has come: The old has gone, the new is here!" (2 Corinthians 5:17). I praise You that

———————————————————————————————————— .

"God decided in advance to adopt us into his own family by bringing us to himself through Jesus Christ. This is what he wanted to do, and it gave him great pleasure" (Ephesians 1:5 NLT). I praise You for

———————————————————————————————————— .

"But now in Christ Jesus you who once were far away have been brought near by the blood of Christ" (Ephesians 2:13). Thank You that

———————————————————————————————————— .

I am so grateful to be welcomed into Your family as Your daughter. When I think I should be excluded, that I am not welcome, or I am not good enough, reassure me of my place through Your kindness and goodness. Amen.

UNDER GOD'S WINGS

Boaz replied, "I've been told all about what you have done for your mother-in-law since the death of your husband—how you left your father and mother and your homeland and came to live with a people you did not know before. May the LORD repay you for what you have done. May you be richly rewarded by the LORD, the God of Israel, under whose wings you have come to take refuge."

RUTH 2:11–12

Ruth's reputation had gone before her. The people in the town had not only been stirred by Naomi's appearance; Ruth had made an impression too.

Boaz had been told about Ruth. Ruth's loyalty to bitter, penniless Naomi was the reason she, a foreigner, picked up leftover stalks of barley in his field. Boaz knew this foreign Moabite woman had left the security of home to travel to a country she didn't know and to live among a people she didn't know. Boaz also knew Ruth had put her trust in God. At a time when God's people were choosing to worship foreign gods, Ruth had decided to follow the one true God.

Boaz also knew that God notices good deeds and rewards people for their kindness. Ruth, a foreigner, was displaying the principles God expected from His people. Yet reward wasn't the reason for Ruth's kindness to Naomi; it was because Ruth had made a genuine decision of devotion to Naomi and, at the same time, taken a risk of going all in with God.

Whereas Ruth invoked God's punishment on herself if she did not follow through on her commitment to Naomi,[a] Boaz prayed for blessings and the same kindness Ruth had shown to Naomi.

Ruth had come under the protective wings of God. Those wings came in the form of a godly man following God's laws who protected and provided for her. Likewise Rahab, also a foreign woman, came under God's protection through the community of the Israelites.

It's the same for you. When you make a commitment to God, you come under His protection. You are safe under the wings of God. You may not know for certain what that protection will look like, but you can be assured that God will provide all you need.

Asking for and acknowledging protection under God's wings is a familiar theme in the Psalms. Use one or more of these verses from the Psalms as your prayer to either praise or plead to know God's safekeeping.

Lord God,

"Keep me as the apple of your eye; hide me in the shadow of your wings" (Psalm 17:8). As Your precious daughter, keep me from the harm of

---

--- .

"Have mercy on me, O God, have mercy! I look to you for protection. I will hide beneath the shadow of your wings" (Psalm 57:1 NLT). Be kind to me and forgive me for

---

--- .

[a] [Ruth said,] "Where you die I will die, and there I will be buried. May the LORD deal with me, be it ever so severely, if even death separates you and me" (Ruth 1:17).

"For you have been my refuge, a strong tower against the foe. I long to dwell in your tent forever and take refuge in the shelter of your wings" (Psalm 61:3–4). I praise and thank You for Your past protection of

_____

_____

_____ .

"Because you are my helper, I sing for joy in the shadow of your wings" (Psalm 63:7 NLT). May I never stop knowing the joy of

_____

_____

_____ .

"He will cover you with his feathers. He will shelter you with his wings. His faithful promises are your armor and protection. Do not be afraid of the terrors of the night, nor the arrow that flies in the day" (Psalm 91:4–5 NLT). I praise You because You give me sufficient protection and rest from

_____

_____

_____ .

Amen.

DAY 88

A COMMITMENT
TO EXCELLENCE

So Ruth gleaned in the field until evening. Then she threshed the barley
she had gathered, and it amounted to about an ephah. She carried it
back to town, and her mother-in-law saw how much she had gathered.
Ruth also brought out and gave her what she had left over after she
had eaten enough.

RUTH 2:17–18

Gleaning, picking up individual stalks of barley, was backbreaking work.
Then, as the sun set, Ruth began threshing the stalks, trampling the grain
until the head of grain separated from the chaff.

Day in, day out, Ruth went to the fields to provide for her mother-in-law and herself.

Ruth's work reminds us of the woman of excellence described in Proverbs
31. Here is a selection of the work she does: She is like the merchant ships,
bringing her food from afar. She gets up while it is still night; she provides
food for her family and portions for her female servants. She sets about
her work vigorously; her arms are strong for her tasks. She opens her arms
to the poor and extends her hands to the needy. And she fears the LORD.

Ruth's determination extended to all areas of her life—from the spiritual
"Your God [will be] my God" (Ruth 1:16), to the physical "Where you
go I will go" (v. 16), to the practical, diligence in working hard to provide
food for Naomi and herself. She took advantage of the generosity of Boaz
and the opportunities he provided. She made the most of God's stipulations
and His provisions for the poor, widow, and foreigner.

Throughout the Bible, working hard is commended. God worked as Creator and saw that His work was good. Jesus worked as a carpenter. Paul and
many early Christians worked in different professions as well as in ministry.

229

Our commitment in life is more than spiritual devotedness. It is to work and provide for ourselves with excellence. God does provide for us and we are always invited to put our hope in Him. But at the same time, we are to put our faith into practice, to be known for our excellence, whether it is providing for ourselves, for our families, and for those in trouble, or whether it is devoting ourselves to good deeds.[a]

Where God has provided, use what He has given you to provide for yourself and for others. Today, pray for the work that you do. Make a commitment to do it with excellence.

[a] Read 1 Timothy 5:3–10.

Lord God, I want to do my work with sincerity of heart and reverence to You. I commit to managing everything I do with excellence. I commit to being diligent in providing for myself and (name others you are responsible for)

_____

_____

and (write down some practical ways and areas in which you want to be excellent)

_____

_____

_____ .

I commit to being generous to those who are in trouble or in need by (spend a few minutes thinking of one or two ways you can respond to needs that come to your attention, whether at home, in your community, or globally)

_____

_____ .

Amen.

COMMITTED TO BEING COURAGEOUS

When Boaz had finished eating and drinking and was in good spirits, he went over to lie down at the far end of the grain pile. Ruth approached quietly, uncovered his feet and lay down. In the middle of the night something startled the man; he turned— and there was a woman lying at his feet! "Who are you?" he asked. "I am your servant Ruth," she said. "Spread the corner of your garment over me, since you are a guardian-redeemer of our family."

RUTH 3:7–9

Harvesting had finished, the hard work of threshing had been completed. Boaz slept, and yet he was startled in the middle of the night by Ruth at his feet.

Naomi had explained to Ruth that she needed to find a home for Ruth where she would be provided for in the future.[a] Naomi came up with a plan, and Ruth agreed to do exactly what Naomi told her.[b]

Lying down at the feet of Boaz in the middle of the night was a brave move. Previously she had not valued herself as worthy enough to be seen as a servant to Boaz. Here, her actions signified a request for Boaz as guardian-redeemer to marry her. Ruth was asking Boaz to take her under his wings and assume responsibility to care and protect her. As a guardian-redeemer, Boaz would also purchase all the property of Elimelek, Kilion, and Mahlon and "purchase" Ruth as his wife.

[a] One day Ruth's mother-in-law Naomi said to her, "My daughter, I must find a home for you, where you will be well provided for" (Ruth 3:1).

[b] "I will do whatever you say," Ruth answered. So she went down to the threshing floor and did everything her mother-in-law told her to do (Ruth 3:5).

231

Perhaps Ruth's request, "spread the corner of your garment over me" (Ruth 3:9), reminded Boaz of his prayer for Ruth: "May you be richly rewarded by the LORD, the God of Israel, under whose wings you have come to take refuge" (2:12).

Boaz had prayed that the God of Israel would reward Ruth for her commitment to Naomi and to God. Now God answered that prayer by Boaz himself.

We discovered with Naomi on day 83 that Jesus is our redeemer. It is through our faith in Jesus that, we receive protection under God's wings. Thank God for the protection you receive for eternity because of Jesus.

Lord God, as I seek shelter under Your wings, I praise You and thank You for purchasing my life with the life of Your Son, Jesus Christ. (Use the following verses to praise and thank God in your own words.)

"He is so rich in kindness and grace that he purchased our freedom with the blood of his Son and forgave our sins. . . .

"And when you believed in Christ, he identified you as his own by giving you the Holy Spirit, whom he promised long ago. The Spirit is God's guarantee that he will give us the inheritance he promised and that he has purchased us to be his own people. He did this so we would praise and glorify him" (Ephesians 1:7, 13–14 NLT). I thank You and praise You for

_____

_____

_____

_____ .

"For everyone has sinned; we all fall short of God's glorious standard. Yet God, in his grace, freely makes us right in his sight. He did this through

Christ Jesus when he freed us from the penalty for our sins" (Romans 3:23–24 NLT). I thank You for

_____

_____

_____

_____

"For God bought you with a high price. So you must honor God with your body" (1 Corinthians 6:20 NLT). I honor You by

_____

_____

_____

_____

Amen.

COMMITMENT TO OTHERS

"The LORD bless you, my daughter," he replied. "This kindness is greater than that which you showed earlier: You have not run after the younger men, whether rich or poor."

RUTH 3:10

Boaz's reply seems strange. Yet in asking Boaz to marry her and finding protection for herself, Ruth was thinking of Naomi, and Boaz recognized and commended Ruth's kindness to Naomi.

Naomi's plan, in kindness to Ruth, was to find her a husband who could give Ruth a home. Ruth, however, had gone through with the plan in kindness to Naomi because Boaz was Naomi's guardian-redeemer too. In this way, Ruth's act of asking Boaz to marry her was greater than the kindness of coming to Bethlehem with Naomi.

Boaz was a noble man, and he told Ruth he would do as she asked. Ruth would make an equally noble wife for him.

All along, Ruth had been thinking of Naomi more than herself. The commitment she made on the road to Bethlehem did not waver but would continue until she had found long-term security for Naomi.

We have been assured that God provides for us. He provides for our day-to-day needs, and He provides for our future with Him through Jesus Christ.

When we know we are secure in God and Christ, we too can seek the security of others.

We prayed to be women of excellence in our work; let's pray to go one step further and be excellent in our work of showing God's kindness to other people and telling them about Jesus. We began our look at Ruth on day 84 by praying to be committed to God; now we are going to pray to be committed to other people. It reminds us of the most important commandments we are to follow: "'Love the Lord your God with all your heart

and with all your soul and with all your strength and with all your mind';
and, 'Love your neighbor as yourself'" (Luke 10:27).

Pray about the people in your life who need to know about God's kindness and to whom you can show personal kindness.

Lord God, thank You for Your kindness shown to me. I understand that Your kindness is not just for myself but so I can show others kindness and that You are kind to them also. May I show unwavering devotion to (name people you love)

_____

_____ .

May I be faithful in my responsibility to (name people you are in charge of or care for)

_____ .

May I be an example of Your kindness and so share the love of Jesus with (name people who need to know Jesus)

_____

_____ .

Amen.

COMMITTED TO WAITING

When Ruth came to her mother-in-law, Naomi asked, "How did it go, my daughter?" Then she told her everything Boaz had done for her and added, "He gave me these six measures of barley, saying, 'Don't go back to your mother-in-law empty-handed.'" Then Naomi said, "Wait, my daughter, until you find out what happens. For the man will not rest until the matter is settled today."

RUTH 3:16–18

Boaz had committed to Ruth's request, but there was a problem: "Although it is true that I am a guardian-redeemer of our family, there is another who is more closely related than I. Stay here for the night, and in the morning if he wants to do his duty as your guardian-redeemer, good; let him redeem you. But if he is not willing, as surely as the LORD lives I will do it" (Ruth 3:12–13).

Ruth and Naomi had to wait until Boaz approached the closer relative to see if he wanted to redeem the land of Naomi's husband and take Ruth for his wife. To reassure Ruth and Naomi of his intentions to marry Ruth, Boaz sent them a gift of barley. This reassured Naomi that Boaz would not rest until the matter was settled. But in the meantime, Ruth had to *wait*. The Hebrew word for *wait* means to "sit down." Ruth could relax confidently knowing that Boaz would follow through on his commitment.

Often we wait impatiently. Sitting down is the last thing we do. Typically, we pace the floor. Waiting for God is usually the same. We wait nervously wondering if God will or won't answer our prayers. However, in our waiting, we too can have confidence in God. We know that God promises to protect us and provide for us. It is not a matter of *if* He will do those things; it is just a matter of when.

We have also learned that with God's provision, we lack no good thing

(Psalm 34:10). You have taken shelter under God's wings, and like Ruth, you can rest. Even in the waiting, God will provide all you need.

Today, as you wait for God, ask Him to give you reassurance in the waiting. Look for His generosity toward you throughout your day.

Lord God, these are the things I am waiting for, including the prayers I am waiting for You to answer:

_____

_____

_____

_____

This is why I find it hard to wait and I get impatient:

_____

_____

I ask for Your reassurance as I hope in You. Remind me today that I can have confidence in You, that You will provide for my needs even while I am waiting. (Look for God's generosity toward you throughout your day, then come back and write down how He has provided for you and given you reassurance.)

_____

_____

Amen.

COMMITMENT FROM OTHERS

> Today you are witnesses that I have bought from Naomi all the property of Elimelek, Kilion and Mahlon. I have also acquired Ruth the Moabite, Mahlon's widow, as my wife, in order to maintain the name of the dead with his property, so that his name will not disappear from among his family or from his hometown.
>
> RUTH 4:9–10

[a] "The witnesses' request concerning Ruth is extraordinary inasmuch as they pray that Yahweh would grant this foreign woman a place among the matriarchs of Israel along with Rachel and Leah."[1]

[b] This, then, is the family line of Perez: Perez was the father of Hezron, Hezron the father of Ram, Ram the father of Amminadab, Amminadab the father of Nahshon, Nahshon the father of Salmon, Salmon the father of Boaz, Boaz the father of Obed, Obed the father of Jesse, and Jesse the father of David (Ruth 4:18–22).

Boaz made his commitment to Ruth, and the people of the town prayed for Ruth and Boaz.

They prayed for Ruth: "May the LORD make the woman who is coming into your home like Rachel and Leah, who together built up the family of Israel" (Ruth 4:11). In doing so they honored Ruth, a Moabite woman, with the request that God establish her alongside the matriarchs of Israel. They prayed that Ruth's children would be comparable to Rachel's and Leah's children in building up the people of Israel, God's people.[a] They asked God to bless Ruth so she would be fruitful.

The people also prayed for Boaz, already a noble man, that he would have a good name and "be famous in Bethlehem" (Ruth 4:11). That through the children he and Ruth had, his family would be "like that of Perez" (Ruth 4:12). Perez was the ancestor of Boaz.[b]

Boaz had taken Ruth as his wife so that the lineage of Ruth's dead husband would continue. However, instead of blessing Mahlon with children, the people of the town prayed for Boaz's family line to continue.

The people of the town had seen Ruth's kindness to Naomi. Now they prayed for God's continued kindness to be shown to Ruth.

We can invite people to pray for us. We should tell them to pray big, bold prayers over us. They can pray in ways that we cannot pray for ourselves. Their prayers can uplift and encourage us, but most of all, we invite them to pray because God "is able to do immeasurably more than all we ask or imagine, according to his power that is at work within us" (Ephesians 3:20).

(Recall from Day 30 the names of people who could encourage, support, and pray for you, and others God might bring to mind now.) Lord God, thank You for the people You've placed in my life who are committed to prayer:

_____   _____

_____   _____

_____   _____

_____   _____

(Commit to asking them to pray boldly for you.)

Amen.

GOD'S KINDNESS

So Boaz took Ruth and she became his wife. When he
made love to her, the LORD enabled her to conceive,
and she gave birth to a son.

RUTH 4:13

ª Obed the father
of Jesse, and Jesse
the father of David
(Ruth 4:22).

Ruth gave birth to a son named Obed. Obed was the
grandfather of David.ª Obed and Boaz are listed in the
genealogies of Jesus in the gospels of Matthew and Luke.
The prayer of the townspeople—"May the LORD make
the woman who is coming into your home like Rachel and
Leah, who together built up the family of Israel. May you
. . . be famous in Bethlehem" (Ruth 4:11)—was answered.

More importantly, Matthew lists Ruth in his genealogy
of Jesus. Only five women are mentioned by Matthew in
the genealogy of Jesus. Rahab is also one of them.

When God gave His regulations for worship to His
people after they had escaped Egypt, God had not permit-
ted a "Moabite or any of their descendants for ten generations" (Deuteronomy 23:3 NLT) to be in the congregation
to worship Him. But here we have a Moabite woman
being recognized as part of the family of Jesus, God's Son.

Ruth and Rahab, foreign women, stand out as not just
accepted but honored. It's remarkable that both of these
women, worshipers of idols who came to God for protection, are rewarded with being in the lineage of Jesus. God's
grace excludes no one from His family.

We might think that Ruth's kindness earned her a position
in the family of God. But it is not about what Ruth had
done but always about God's kindness first and foremost.

It is the same for us. It is not our background or our history that identifies us as worthy or unworthy of God's kindness. It is God's willingness to be gracious to us. When we come to God for protection, our faith puts us in the family of God.

You may have never made an *all-in* commitment with your life to God. We are going to use words from Psalm 63:1, 8: "You, God, are my God, earnestly I seek you; . . . I cling to you; your right hand upholds me," which uses the same word for *cleave* that Ruth used to make her wholehearted commitment. And, if you have been following God faithfully, you can use words from Psalm 119:30–31 to recommit your life to God: "I have chosen to be faithful; I have determined to live by your regulations. I cling to your laws. LORD, don't let me be put to shame!" (NLT).

Fill in the prompts using the words of Psalms 63 and 119, printed above.

Lord God, You are my God. I earnestly (fill in from Psalm 63:1, 8)

_____ You . I _____ to You.

I have chosen to be faithful to You. I have determined to live (fill in from Psalm 119:30–31)

_____

_____ .

(Tell God how you will sincerely and seriously commit to Him like never before.) Lord, I will

_____

_____ .

(Now write down small, practical ways—like starting your day with a prayer or a Bible verse, or making a new commitment you sense God is asking of you—that will help you cling to God with all your strength.) I will cling to you by

_____

_____

_____ .

Amen.

A WOMAN OF STRENGTH
Hannah

Hannah is the wife of Elkanah. Elkanah had another wife called Peninnah. As Hannah is named before Peninnah when listing Elkanah's wives, it is most likely that Hannah was his first wife.[a] With Hannah, we see a familiar problem we have encountered with Sarah, Rebekah, and Rachel. Hannah could not conceive.

Hannah stands out as having a remarkable commitment and understanding of God. She is faithful to God in her life and her worship of God. Scholars believe that Hannah's prayer in 1 Samuel 2 is one of the earliest examples of Israelite poetry. As we enter into Hannah's pain and explore her relationship with God, we learn from an ordinary woman how we should pray and praise God when we are suffering.

[a] There was a certain man from Ramathaim, a Zuphite from the hill country of Ephraim, whose name was Elkanah son of Jeroham, the son of Elihu, the son of Tohu, the son of Zuph, an Ephraimite. He had two wives; one was called Hannah and the other Peninnah (1 Samuel 1:1–2).

SUFFERING AT THE HANDS OF OTHERS

Because the LORD had closed Hannah's womb, her rival kept provoking her in order to irritate her.

1 SAMUEL 1:6

Along with the shame and anxiety of having no children came another familiar issue, that of being taunted by another woman. Peninnah provoked Hannah because of her barrenness. In the same way, Hagar, when she became pregnant with Abraham's child, ridiculed Sarah.

Peninnah had given Elkanah children.[a] Elkanah, however, loved Hannah.

First Samuel 1:4–5 says, "Whenever the day came for Elkanah to sacrifice, he would give portions of the meat to his wife Peninnah and to all her sons and daughters. But to Hannah he gave a double portion because he loved her, and the LORD had closed her womb."

Perhaps Elkanah's favoritism of Hannah caused Peninnah to torment Hannah for her childlessness. Just like with Leah, Peninnah found that producing children was not enough to gain the affection of a husband.

Peninnah's behavior brings up an important issue we often face: relationships that are difficult, confrontational, and damaging to our sense of worth. When we are already struggling with a problem that affects our self-esteem, the last thing we need is for someone else to make us feel worse about ourselves. When we are at the mercy of someone's jealousy and discontentment, through no fault of our own,

[a] He had two wives; one was called Hannah and the other Peninnah. Peninnah had children, but Hannah had none (1 Samuel 1:2).

it can make us feel worn down. Life is often hard enough without other people making it harder. It is easy to react and retaliate to the meanness of other people, but as we have seen with Sarah and Hagar, and with Rachel and Leah, striking back does not resolve problems.

We are going to begin our story of Hannah being determined to be women who—no matter how much we are ridiculed or treated badly by other people—do not take things into our own hands but take our problems to God.

But first, we are going to focus our attention on God and not our problems. We begin by delighting in and praising God for being our Rock, our foundation and source of security and strength.

Lord God, I praise You for being *my rock, my fortress, and my savior . . . in whom I find protection.* You are *my shield, the power that saves me, and my place of safety* (Psalm 18:2 NLT). (Give praise to God in your own words for His care for you.) I praise You

_____

_____

_____ .

I worship *You the Rock; Your deeds are perfect. Everything You do is just and fair. You are a faithful God who does no wrong; just and upright.*[a] (Using your own words, thank God for being completely reliable and trustworthy.) I thank You

[a] Taken from Deuteronomy 32:4 NLT.

_____

_____

_____ .

Amen.

ALONE IN OUR SUFFERING

This went on year after year. Whenever Hannah went up to the house of the LORD, her rival provoked her till she wept and would not eat. Her husband Elkanah would say to her, "Hannah, why are you weeping? Why don't you eat? Why are you downhearted? Don't I mean more to you than ten sons?"

1 SAMUEL 1:7–8

The extra serving of food Elkanah gave Hannah sat uneaten. Instead, tears splashed onto the plate. How Peninnah must have gloated to see Hannah's misery. Hannah had no relief from the torment inflicted by Peninnah. She could not escape from Peninnah, connected as they were as wives of Elkanah.

Yet Peninnah wanted more than to make Hannah cry and lose her appetite. Peninnah's constant taunting was to "irritate" Hannah hugely (1 Samuel 1:6). The word can mean to "humiliate" or "oppress." If Peninnah did succeed in making Hannah angry, we see no evidence of it.

Maybe Elkanah didn't notice the cruel way Peninnah treated Hannah. The jibes of a bully can be subtle. Maybe he did and didn't know how to stop it. Or he chose to ignore it. Certainly Elkanah, as loving as he was toward Hannah, didn't understand her misery.

Suffering can be lonely. Often other people, even those who are closest to us, do not fully understand what we are going through. And sometimes our anxiety and pain are so intense that our bodies react too. We may lose our appetite like Hannah. Or we may eat more to relieve our stress. Maybe you lay awake for hours in the night as you think about all that is worrying you.

What anxiety are you facing at the moment that makes you feel all alone? What is causing you to lay awake at night or messing with your appetite? The Bible says: "Cast all your anxiety on him because he cares for you" (1 Peter 5:7).

We are going to learn more from Hannah about bringing our anxiety to God, but for the moment, tell God what is making you anxious and the reactions you are experiencing.

Lord God, I am anxious about

_____

_____

_____

_____

In my anxiety, I am reacting by (write down your actions and behaviors as a result of your worries)

_____

_____

_____

Amen.

WHEN ONLY GOD CAN HELP

Once when they had finished eating and drinking in Shiloh, Hannah stood up. Now Eli the priest was sitting on his chair by the doorpost of the LORD's house.

1 SAMUEL 1:9

Hannah stood up. It seems like an insignificant action, but it involved a decisive step. Hannah had made the decision that she was going to do something about the misery and shame she was experiencing.

Hannah went to the tabernacle, the portable sanctuary at that time in which God dwelled. Hannah, Elkanah, and Peninnah and her children were already in Shiloh, the location of the tabernacle, to worship and fulfill their annual sacrifice to the Lord.[a] However, Hannah decided to go and seek God on her own.

Hannah stood up and went to God.

Sarah, we learned, took matters into her own hands. She gave Hagar to Abraham so she could have a child (day 11). And when Hagar despised her, she made Hagar's life miserable. Rachel blamed her husband and saw her infertility as a battle with her sister to be won. Rachel gave her servant to Jacob and saw the children Bilhah bore as a victory over her sister (day 39).

Hannah saw her problem as God's business, not anyone else's. It was God who had closed her womb. Hannah didn't confront Peninnah to get the provoking to stop once and

[a] Year after year this man went up from his town to worship and sacrifice to the LORD Almighty at Shiloh (1 Samuel 1:3).

249

for all. Hannah didn't try to get Elkanah to understand. She went to God who would fully understand.

Even when we take our problems to God in prayer, we can be tempted to take matters into our own hands. We decide that we need to fix things. Other times we get angry with those who fail to understand what we are going through. Or we decide they are the reason for our problems and pass the blame. Often, when another person is annoying, frustrating, or even tormenting us, we think the only way to stop them is to confront them.

Where are you taking your pain? Like Hannah, let's commit to taking our problems to God. Let God's words speak to you through the Bible verses in this prayer. Then respond to God with your commitment to depend on Him.

"For I am the LORD your God who takes hold of your right hand and says to you, Do not fear; I will help you" (Isaiah 41:13).

"Don't be afraid, for I am with you. Don't be discouraged, for I am your God. I will strengthen you and help you. I will hold you up with my victorious right hand" (Isaiah 41:10 NLT).

"Come to me, all you who are weary and burdened, and I will give you rest" (Matthew 11:28).

"Keep on asking, and you will receive what you ask for. Keep on seeking, and you will find. Keep on knocking, and the door will be opened to you" (Matthew 7:7 NLT).

Amen.

OUR TEARS ARE OUR PRAYERS

In her deep anguish Hannah prayed to the LORD, weeping bitterly.

1 SAMUEL 1:10

Hannah wept "bitterly" (1 Samuel 1:10). All the stress, anger, hurt, and resentment of Peninnah being mean to her came pouring out. Hannah wept bitterly because God had closed her womb. Like Sarah, Hannah could have stated: "The LORD has kept me from having children" (Genesis 16:2). Instead, Hannah knew that if God had closed her womb, He was the only One who could open it.

Like Naomi, Hannah could have said, "The Almighty has made my life very bitter" (Ruth 1:20). Instead, she poured out her bitterness to God. Naomi expressed her misery to other people. Hannah brought her wretchedness to God.

Hannah prayed. Hannah believed that standing in the presence of the sovereign God would stop her from being pushed around by Peninnah. Hannah knew that the Lord Almighty could relieve her deep anguish.

Our tears can be our prayers. Pouring out our pain to God *is* prayer.

Express the cries of your heart in your own words using Psalm 102 as your prayer.

Lord God, *Hear my prayer, LORD; let my cry for help come to you. Do not hide your face from me when I am in distress* (vv. 1–2). (Write down the pain you are experiencing.)

_____

_____

Turn your ear to me; when I call, answer me quickly (v. 2). (Write down the prayers you have been waiting for God to answer.)

_____

_____ .

In my distress I groan aloud (v. 5). (Write down the sorrow and sadness you feel.)

_____

_____ .

But you, LORD, sit enthroned forever . . . You will arise and have compassion (v. 12). Amen.

THE LORD ALMIGHTY

> And she made a vow, saying, "LORD Almighty, if you will only look on your servant's misery and remember me, and not forget your servant but give her a son, then I will give him to the LORD for all the days of his life, and no razor will ever be used on his head."
>
> 1 SAMUEL 1:11

Hannah made a vow, a sincere promise to God, that she would dedicate her child to God. Dedicating someone to the service of God for a period of time was not unusual.[a] But Hannah decided she would give her child to God for his entire life in gratitude for answering her prayer.

Hannah's prayer and solemn promise began with the recognition of God as "LORD Almighty" (1 Samuel 1:11). She recognized God had sovereign power over her barrenness. That's why she poured out her heart to him and no one else, not Eli the priest, not her husband, and certainly not Peninnah. God, the Lord Almighty, the Giver of life, the Creator of all life, could bring life from her dead womb.

Hannah called herself a "servant" twice (v. 11). She had respect for God because He was Lord of her life. Her words imply submission to God. He didn't have to do what she wanted, so she would be humble in her asking. The word *servant* in Hebrew is the same word used for a female slave. Slaves were required to do everything their masters and mistresses ordered. Yet Hannah volunteered herself to be in absolute subjection to her Lord, to serve

[a] Read Leviticus 27:1–8.

Him in every way she could. Hannah did not see herself as a victim of her circumstances but accepted whatever God ordained for her life.

Yet at the same time, Hannah petitioned God to change her circumstances. She asked Him to "remember" and "not forget" (v. 11). *Remember*, we discovered with Rachel (day 94), means that God is active in being faithful to His promises.

Hannah teaches us that we find strength when we pour out our pain to the One who is Lord over our problems. Strength comes from submitting to God in His sovereign power and believing He can and is willing to turn around our situations. Strength comes from knowing God will remember us because He is faithful.

Lord Almighty, You are sovereign over

_____

_____ .

As Your servant, I ask You to remember me, because You are faithful, and answer my prayer of

_____

_____ .

I will trust You with the outcome. Amen.

POURING OUT OUR PAIN

As she kept on praying to the LORD, Eli observed her mouth. Hannah was praying in her heart, and her lips were moving but her voice was not heard. Eli thought she was drunk and said to her, "How long are you going to stay drunk? Put away your wine." "Not so, my lord," Hannah replied, "I am a woman who is deeply troubled. I have not been drinking wine or beer; I was pouring out my soul to the LORD. Do not take your servant for a wicked woman; I have been praying here out of my great anguish and grief."

1 SAMUEL 1:12–16

Hannah "kept on praying" (1 Samuel 1:12). She did not give up.

Hannah prayed in her heart. She praying silently, pouring out her soul to the Lord. But Eli the priest thought she was drunk. Drunk people stagger and sway. They struggle to keep their balance, and they are noisy. Hannah's approach to prayer might not have looked appropriate to Eli, yet we know she wasn't being disrespectful in the presence of God. She had humbly called herself the Lord's servant.

In Hannah's reply to Eli, we see her deep humility. She said: "Do not take your servant for a wicked woman" (1 Samuel 1:16). The term for "wicked woman" here is "daughter of Belial," a phrase suggesting one who failed to give due respect to God.[a] Hannah was saying: I am not failing to give respect to God.

[a] "The phrase ['wicked woman'] suggests one who failed to give due respect to God or others and who therefore represented a threat to proper religious and societal order."[1]

256

Pouring out our pain to God can look messy and far from respectable. Yet we keep coming back to prayer, having faith that God is able to do all that we ask. While God may not answer our prayers in the way we want or on the timeline we'd like, God will hear us in our humble submission to Him.

Jesus prayed like Hannah too: While Jesus was here on earth, He offered prayers and pleadings, with a loud cry and tears, to the One who could rescue Him from death. And God heard His prayers because of His deep reverence for God (Hebrews 5:7 NLT).

Come back to God again and plead with Him, with a focus on your willingness to submit to Him.

Lord Almighty, I come back to You again with my prayer of pain. I ask (write down ways in which you want God to answer)

_____

_____

_____ .

I am trusting You with the answer whether it is yes, no, or not yet, in humble surrender to Your will for my life. (Talk to God using the verses below about your willingness, or struggle, to accept His answer and submit to Him.)

"I take joy in doing your will, my God, for your instructions are written on my heart" (Psalm 40:8 NLT).

_____

_____ .

"Teach me to do your will, for you are my God. May your gracious Spirit lead me forward on a firm footing" (Psalm 143:10 NLT).

_____

_____ .

Amen.

FINDING GOD'S PEACE

Eli answered, "Go in peace, and may the God of Israel grant you what you have asked of him." She said, "May your servant find favor in your eyes." Then she went her way and ate something, and her face was no longer downcast.

1 Samuel 1:17–18

Hannah's prayers had been worthwhile. Her prayer has not even been answered, but Hannah was at peace. She had regained her appetite. Her load felt lighter.

Eli, having thought Hannah was a "wicked woman," also sent Hannah on her way with a prayer to know God's peace.

Hannah went back to exactly the same situation she had left. She was not pregnant. Peninnah was still there to taunt her mercilessly. However, Hannah's time with God, pouring out her pain, had transformed her. Perhaps Hannah couldn't smile yet, but the anguish had left her.

Prayer makes a difference in our lives. The purpose of pouring out the pain is so we can find peace. We want our prayers to be answered but more important is finding a restfulness for our hearts and minds, a peace which "exceeds anything we can understand" (Philippians 4:7 NLT). God's peace is restfulness that is promised as a result of our passionate prayers. Philippians 4:6 says: "Do not be anxious about anything, but in every situation, by prayer and petition, with thanksgiving, present your requests to God." Passionate prayer and peace go hand in hand.

You have wept bitterly before God. You have made your request. Keep coming back to God until you receive His peace. Remember He promises to give you calm in the chaos.

Lord God, I thank You for the promise of peace, regardless of the answer to my prayers. I ask You to exchange my pain for peace. I ask You to be faithful to Your promises of giving me a calmness and restfulness in all my circumstances. In particular I ask You . . .

"In peace I will lie down and sleep, for you alone, O LORD, will keep me safe" (Psalm 4:8 NLT). When I can't sleep

"The LORD gives strength to his people; the LORD blesses his people with peace" (Psalm 29:11). When I'm feeling physically or emotionally weak

"But the meek will inherit the land and enjoy peace and prosperity" (Psalm 37:11). When I'm feeling wretched and humiliated

"Those who love your instructions have great peace and do not stumble" (Psalm 119:165 NLT). When I've made mistakes

"He grants peace to your borders and satisfies you with the finest of wheat" (Psalm 147:14). When I'm fighting with other people

"May you live to enjoy your grandchildren" (Psalm 128:6 NLT). When I'm feeling frail and facing sickness or disease

_____

_____ .

Amen.

ANSWERED PRAYER

Early the next morning they arose and worshiped before the LORD and then went back to their home at Ramah. Elkanah made love to his wife Hannah, and the LORD remembered her. So in the course of time Hannah became pregnant and gave birth to a son. She named him Samuel, saying, "Because I asked the LORD for him."

1 SAMUEL 1:19–20

Hannah worshiped. God had not even answered her prayer at this point. To worship means that Hannah bowed down before God. This is the same posture Hannah has always taken before God. Hannah humbly saw herself as God's servant. Hannah acknowledged God as Lord Almighty, sovereign over everything in her life. All of these positions were an act of worship.

Hannah worshiped God even though He had not answered her request. It is an example to us that even though our prayers are yet to be answered in the way that we think we need, we still worship God. We serve God willingly while we wait. We respectfully recognize that God is Lord over our lives and give Him the praise He is due.

Eventually, God remembered Hannah and her request. God was faithful to her. God had not forgotten Hannah and her vow. God in His perfect timing answered her prayer. The word *remembered* is used when something significant happens (1 Samuel 1:19). Samuel, the child given to Hannah by God, would be a prophet and judge who would anoint both Saul and David as kings.

Philippians 4:6 reminds us that our prayers and requests are to be made with thanksgiving: "Do not be anxious about anything, but in every situation, by prayer and petition, with thanksgiving, present your requests to God."

We are to follow our prayers of requests with prayers of thanksgiving even when our prayers have not been answered. We are to remember the goodness and greatness of God, which can help us as we wait on Him to answer our prayers. We are to worship God every day and every way we can. Use this prayer to praise and worship the Lord God.

Lord God, I come to You in worship. I bow down, I kneel, I lift my hands (do one or more of these before God). With my breath I praise You. (Say the following words out loud.) *You are worthy, our Lord and God, to receive glory and honor and power* (Revelation 4:11). I worship You with gladness and thank You for (write down attributes of God that have spoken to you so far through these devotions)

_____

_____

_____

_____ .

I praise You for Your goodness (thank God for something He has done for you recently)

_____

_____

_____

_____ .

Amen.

GOD IS OUR STRENGTH

> Then Hannah prayed and said: "My heart rejoices in the LORD; in the LORD my horn is lifted high. My mouth boasts over my enemies, for I delight in your deliverance. There is no one holy like the LORD; there is no one besides you; there is no Rock like our God."
>
> 1 SAMUEL 2:1–2

Hannah followed through on her vow. She took her little boy, Samuel, to the tabernacle and gave him to Eli the priest to serve God for his entire life.[a] We can imagine Hannah had a lump in her throat and tears in her eyes as she bent down to kiss Samuel goodbye. However, Hannah stood up and cried out in praise to God.

Hannah's praise contrasts with her weeping for the child she so desperately wanted. Hannah's prayers of pain were mostly private, but her praises were public and eloquent.

Yet at the same time, her praise was personal for what God had done for her. She directed her praise to God, but her words were also for those who were listening.

Everything Hannah brought to God came from her heart. Hannah poured out the despair in her heart when she asked God for a child. Hannah's praise now overflowed from her heart.

Hannah had been silent before her enemy, Peninnah. Never once using her mouth to ridicule her rival. Now Hannah boasted loudly about God's victory over her enemies and delighted in God's deliverance. Hannah gave God the glory. God had given her the courage to be exuberant. Not

[a] After he was weaned, she took the boy with her, young as he was, along with a three-year-old bull, an ephah of flour and a skin of wine, and brought him to the house of the LORD at Shiloh (1 Samuel 1:24).

to brag about herself but to praise God. It was not self-congratulations about what she had done, as we saw with Rachel and Leah, but applause for what God had done. Hannah's example is a reminder that our mouths are for praising God, not tearing others apart. We are not to use our mouths to ridicule others who are made in the image of God or declare victory over them.

We are to use our words to praise God.

Hannah bowed her head in pain before God as His humble servant. Now God enabled her to hold her head up high. God was her source of strength because He was "the Rock, his works are perfect, and all his ways are just. A faithful God who does no wrong, upright and just is he" (Deuteronomy 32:4).

It's easier to praise when God has answered our prayers. More importantly, we should praise Him because He answers prayers. We have learned from Hannah that even when our prayers are yet to be answered in the way that we want, we are to praise God (day 101).

This is a reminder to us. We draw strength from God, the One who can deliver us from our painful circumstances. It is God who can raise us up before our "enemies." God is our Rock too. He is perfect, and we can trust Him because He is just and fair.

When we share our stories of pain, let's make sure we also share our praise in God. Giving praise to God puts our problems in perspective. God is sovereign over our lives. When we give praise to God for what He has done or He has not done, we are declaring to other people that God is greater than our problems.

[a] Based on Psalm 71:8.

Lord God, may my mouth be filled with praise for You, declaring Your splendor all day long.[a] May I boast about You when You answer my prayers; may I boast about You even while I am waiting for my prayers to be answered.

(Boast about God's ways and wisdom below, knowing that whatever season you're in, God cares for you.)

_____

_____

_____

_____

_____ .

(Look back at your prayer on day 100. Choose the relevant circumstances to now praise God in.)

When I cannot sleep, *I will sing of your strength, in the morning* (Psalm 59:16) for

_____

_____ .

When I am weak, *you are my strength, I sing praise to you; you, God, are my fortress, my God on whom I can rely* (Psalm 59:17) because

_____

_____ .

When I am wretched and humiliated, I hold onto the truth that *the LORD takes delight in his people; he crowns the humble with victory* (Psalm 149:4). You will

_____

_____ .

When I stumble, *it is God who arms me with strength and keeps my way secure* (Psalm 18:32) and

_____

_____ .

When I am fighting, I stand on Your Word, which says, *He strengthens the bars of your gates and blesses your people within you* (Psalm 147:13). You will

_____

_____ .

When I am frail, *my flesh and my heart may fail, but God is the strength of my heart and my portion forever* (Psalm 73:26). I will praise You

_____

_____ .

Amen.

GOD WHO REVERSES CIRCUMSTANCES

Do not keep talking so proudly or let your mouth speak such arrogance, for the LORD is a God who knows, and by him deeds are weighed. The bows of the warriors are broken, but those who stumbled are armed with strength.

1 SAMUEL 2:3–4

We cannot help but think Hannah was directing these words toward Peninnah. Not to get back at Peninnah but to inform Peninnah of the truths about God. Hannah's words were a warning to Peninnah to rethink the way she thought and spoke.

Yet again we see that God takes the words we say and the things we do seriously. Nothing misses God's attention. Hannah knew that God weighs the deeds, both good and bad, of people and humbles and exalts depending on those deeds.

Hannah also knew that God is the One who reverses circumstances. God had reversed Hannah's circumstances. "She who was barren has borne seven children," said Hannah (1 Samuel 2:5). She had been humble in asking for one child, and God made her feel like she had seven children, the number of completeness.

Hannah said God "raises the poor from the dust and lifts the needy from the ash heap" (v. 8). It makes us think of Hagar (day 22). Hannah said God seats them with princes and has them inherit a throne of honor. It makes us think of Sarah (day 13). God is the One who can reverse our circumstances too.

We can be reassured that God weighs the deeds of those who do wrong to us. We can be reassured that God weighs our deeds when we are humble before Him. As Hannah said, "He will guard the feet of his faithful servants" (v. 9).

We go to God because He is worthy of our honor, but we also go to Him because He is able to answer our prayers and reverse our circumstances. He takes us from guilty to clean when we believe in His Son. He lifts up our heads when we bow before Him. He turns around our lives when He answers our prayers. Thank God for one or more ways He has turned around your life, reversed your circumstances.

Lord God, I thank You for turning around my life. (Choose one or more ways God has reversed your circumstances. Here are some suggestions: healed a relationship [Malachi 4:6], given you a new heart [Ezekiel 36:26], forgiven you [2 Chronicles 7:14], brought health and healing [Jeremiah 33:6], restored your life [Joel 2:25], revived your joy [Psalm 51:12], removed your shame [Isaiah 61:7].) Thank You for

_____

_____

_____

_____

_____

_____

Amen.

GOD OUR ROCK

But Samuel was ministering before the LORD—a boy wearing a linen ephod. Each year his mother made him a little robe and took it to him when she went up with her husband to offer the annual sacrifice. Eli would bless Elkanah and his wife, saying, "May the LORD give you children by this woman to take the place of the one she prayed for and gave to the LORD." Then they would go home. And the LORD was gracious to Hannah; she gave birth to three sons and two daughters. Meanwhile, the boy Samuel grew up in the presence of the LORD.

1 SAMUEL 2:18–21

Hannah's name means "grace," and God was gracious to her (1 Samuel 2:21). The Bible speaks in the same way about God visiting and being gracious to Sarah when she became pregnant with Isaac (Genesis 21:1).

We can imagine Hannah carefully sewing a coat for Samuel each year, wondering if she had made it the right size. Would the sleeves be too short? Would he have grown more than she thought?

Hannah gave her only child, the little boy she had prayed for so passionately at the tabernacle, to work in service to God. Yet God gave her five more children. I'm sure they never filled the hole in her heart for Samuel, but they would have kept her busy enough that she would have had little time to pine.

We have learned from Hannah how to come to God baring all and expose our pain and the distress of our lives. We do this again and again because through our prayers we are promised peace.

We believe, like Hannah, that we bring any and every problem to God because He is Lord, sovereign over everything in our lives. He is the One who can reverse our circumstances. God gives and we can, like Hannah, give back to Him what He has given us.

Hannah's faith didn't get stronger because God answered her prayer.

She had a solid foundation of knowledge and trust in God's goodness and graciousness. We too can have a bedrock of faith and trust in God. However our circumstances change, we can trust God because He remains faithful and true. However we feel, we worship God because He is sovereign.

We began our time with Hannah by praising God for being rock solid. Are you ready to continue trusting God with everything in your life? Let's be women who encourage each other to believe "there is no Rock like our God" (1 Samuel 2:2). Make Hannah's words and your own words your prayer to commit to God your Rock.

Lord God, thank You for being gracious to me in many ways. (Write down how God has generously provided what you need.)

_____

_____ .

I commit to giving back to You in thanksgiving for all You have given me. (Write down one way in which you can give back to God, whether it is financial, your time, possessions . . .)

_____

_____

_____ .

Where I have plenty, may I share freely with others and give generously to those in need. (Write down one way you can be generous.)

_____

_____

_____ .

There is no one besides You. There is no Rock like You. Amen.

A WOMAN WITH GOOD SENSE
Abigail

Abigail lived during the reign of King Saul. David had been anointed by Samuel to be the next king. However, David was living as a fugitive on the run from King Saul who pursued him to take his life. Abigail was married to a very wealthy man named Nabal, who was described as surly and mean in his dealings.

Abigail stood in complete contrast to her husband. She was intelligent, understanding, and discerning. She had qualities we can aspire to and cultivate, especially for averting difficult or explosive situations.

SENSE TO LISTEN

One of the servants told Abigail, Nabal's wife, "David sent messengers from the wilderness to give our master his greetings, but he hurled insults at them. Yet these men were very good to us. They did not mistreat us, and the whole time we were out in the fields near them nothing was missing. Night and day they were a wall around us the whole time we were herding our sheep near them. Now think it over and see what you can do, because disaster is hanging over our master and his whole household. He is such a wicked man that no one can talk to him."

1 SAMUEL 25:14–17

Abigail was a good listener. Not only that, the servant could confide in Abigail, unlike Nabal, Abigail's husband.

Abigail paid attention to the story. She heard the complaint about her husband who had said: "Who is this David? Who is this son of Jesse? Many servants are breaking away from their masters these days. Why should I take my bread and water, and the meat I have slaughtered for my shearers, and give it to men coming from who knows where?" (1 Samuel 25:10–11).

Abigail was attentive to the reason for the complaint, that David's men had been protective of her husband's staff and only wanted provisions to sustain them in return.

The servant requested Abigail use her wisdom. He knew she would respond astutely with good judgment. Her reputation was far better than her husband's.

From the servant's words, Abigail did not need to enter into a dialogue with the servant to determine her conclusion. She had enough information to make a reasoned decision on what to do, while the servant was powerless to change what had already happened.

Abigail stood in complete contrast to her husband. Being known as a woman who can be approached in the middle of a conflict or pending disaster is valuable. If we are going to intervene in a conflict—whether at home, work, or elsewhere—the first step is to listen. Great listeners allow others to be heard. Listening and wisdom go together in the Bible. The Bible invites us to listen well. Proverbs 2:2 says: "turning your ear to wisdom and applying your heart to understanding." Listening is a sign of wisdom: "Let the wise listen and add to their learning" (Proverbs 1:5).

Let's pray to be known as women who listen well not only to other people but especially to God and His words.

Lord God, as I think about conflicts in my life, past, present, and future, I realize that listening is key in all disputes.

First and foremost, I turn my mind and ears to You. I want to be attentive to Your wisdom. May I always remember that trust in You gives me a foundation of wisdom. Turning and listening to You means I will grow in wisdom. I commit to trusting You when I face a conflict by

_____

_____

_____ .

I also ask You to give me the wisdom to listen well to other people, particularly when tempers are flaring and words are being thrown around. May I (pick one of these tendencies or write in your own words what you should work on: pay attention, show I am listening, not jump to conclusions, not interrupt, not think what I have to say is more important than what they have to say)

_____

_____ .

Amen.

SENSE TO RESPOND WELL

Abigail acted quickly. She took two hundred loaves of bread, two skins of wine, five dressed sheep, five seahs of roasted grain, a hundred cakes of raisins and two hundred cakes of pressed figs, and loaded them on donkeys. Then she told her servants, "Go on ahead; I'll follow you." But she did not tell her husband Nabal.

1 SAMUEL 25:18–19

Abigail prepared a feast for David and his men. David had asked Nabal to "be favorable toward my men, since we come at a festive time. Please give your servants and your son David whatever you can find for them" (1 Samuel 25:8). Nabal gave them nothing.

Sheep-shearing season was a festive time of celebration. Being generous was easy for Abigail. With plenty of food on hand, Abigail wasted no time in a critical situation, certainly not going to Nabal to get him to change his mind.

Abigail prepared a generous supply of food for David and his men. She jumped into action to fulfill David's request, and in response to his kindness in providing protection.

Abigail took a risk going behind her husband's back, but maybe she sensed the wrath of a fighting man and his army would be worse than her husband's.

Knowing how to respond in a critical situation is important. Let's be like Abigail and not waste time on arguments but jump into action where necessary. Knowing exactly how to respond can be difficult, but being generous, going above and beyond what was originally asked or expected, is key. Proverbs 11:25 says: "A generous person will prosper; whoever refreshes others will be refreshed." When we think in terms of being openhanded with our responses and breathing new life into situations, we will find the wisdom for any circumstance.

Let's be women who are generous, repaying kindness with kindness. Sometimes we waste time trying to change other people when we should jump into action ourselves to avert a disaster.

Pray for wisdom today to act quickly, wisely, and generously.

Lord God, help me to realize when I should be generous, jumping into action to repay kindness with kindness.

May I remember that You are a generous God. As James 1:5 says, *If any of you lacks wisdom, you should ask God, who gives generously to all without finding fault, and it will be given to you.* (In your own words, thank God for His generosity.)

----- .

I ask for Your wisdom to be openhanded with my words, advice, belongings, finances, or (write in your own words how you can act generously)

----- .

Amen.

DAY 107

SENSE TO BE HUMBLE

Then she told her servants, "Go on ahead; I'll follow you." But she did
not tell her husband Nabal. . . . When Abigail saw David, she quickly
got off her donkey and bowed down before David with her face to the
ground. She fell at his feet and said: "Pardon your servant, my lord,
and let me speak to you; hear what your servant has to say."

1 SAMUEL 25:19, 23–24

Abigail herself took the food to David, although she did send it on ahead.
David would have seen the provisions before he saw Abigail. David,
however, was so focused on the insult he had received and on taking revenge, food alone would probably not have been enough to cool his anger.

Before Abigail spoke a word, she bowed to the ground before David—a
sign of humility, deep respect, and a plea for mercy. In her first words, she
called herself a servant, although as mistress of a household, she was way
above such a lowly position. "Pardon your servant" (1 Samuel 25:24) was
not a polite introduction but a request for forgiveness. Her humility was
the opposite of Nabal's pride and arrogance.

In front of her was a battle-scarred warrior with his sword already
strapped to his side. Enraged by how Nabal had responded, David was
clearly in no mood for negotiation. But with wisdom and tact, Abigail
asked him to listen.

Abigail gives us a picture of how to be nonconfrontational in a situation
fraught with anger and hostility. The gift of food let David know he had
been heard. She understood his position and his request. She also established
his authority above her own.

Often in a heated situation, when words are flying, listening is not on
an angry person's mind. We have to let them know they are heard. We
have to show respect, and we have to reaffirm the other person's position.
We have to take the first step in being humble and taking responsibility

277

for our mistakes. Having empathy doesn't mean we have to agree with the other person, but it does empower us to walk in their shoes and see things from their perspective. We need to do these things before presenting any argument or making a request.

Pray for wisdom today to begin with humility when attempting to diffuse a tense situation.

Lord God, when I face a situation that is fraught with anger and hostility, I realize that having empathy, seeing the situation from the other person's perspective, goes a long way.

May I remember that Your Word tells me that wisdom and humility go hand in hand: *Pride leads to disgrace, but with humility comes wisdom* (Proverbs 11:2 NLT).

I ask You to give me the wisdom to be open-minded, compassionate, respectful, gentle (write in your own words how you can be humble)

_____

_____ .

Forgive me where I have been arrogant, filled with my own self-importance, scornful, or disrespectful (write in your own words how you have been prideful)

_____

_____ .

Give me the sense to know that humility can go a long way to divert an argument or fight. Amen.

SENSE TO HELP OTHERS AVOID REVENGE

Please pay no attention, my lord, to that wicked man Nabal. He is just like his name—his name means Fool, and folly goes with him. And as for me, your servant, I did not see the men my lord sent. And now, my lord, as surely as the LORD your God lives and as you live, since the LORD has kept you from bloodshed and from avenging yourself with your own hands, may your enemies and all who are intent on harming my lord be like Nabal. And let this gift, which your servant has brought to my lord, be given to the men who follow you.

1 SAMUEL 25:25–27

Abigail had earned the right to have David's attention. Only then did she speak. Abigail's speech is one of the longest by a woman recorded in the Old Testament.

"Pay no attention," Abigail tells David to ignore exactly the person David couldn't stop thinking about, Nabal who had insulted him (1 Samuel 25:10–11). Abigail is blunt about her husband. In other words, she knew Nabal's response was not right. She does blame Nabal, but not to honor herself. She stated what was true about her husband and doesn't excuse him, but also takes the blame herself for not seeing David's men when they arrived. Abigail wanted to divert David's attention away from Nabal and to draw attention to the fact that it was not worth spending his time on a fool.

She pointed out that God had kept David from avenging himself—"since the LORD has kept you from bloodshed and from avenging yourself with your own hands" (v. 26). Perhaps Abigail was implying that God had sent her to intervene because David hadn't yet taken revenge on Nabal. Perhaps her words made David think, because David feared God. She prayed that all David's enemies would be like Nabal, foolish. She knew that "the fear of the LORD is the beginning of knowledge, but fools despise wisdom and instruction" (Proverbs 1:7). Fools, she knew, "hated knowledge and did not choose to fear the LORD" (Proverbs 1:29).

We are wise to divert people's attention away from those who, through their insults, are a waste of time and to direct their attention toward bigger and more important topics than taking matters into their own hands. We have seen the damage so far with Sarah, Rebekah, Rachel, and Leah of taking things into our own hands. We have prayed that we may seek God's guidance. Now we are encouraged to help others do the same.

Lord God, as I step into a situation where I can see a person is not managing a conflict well, I realize that intervening takes wisdom.

May I earn the right to speak because I have sought Your wisdom (fill in with your commitment to listen to God from day 105)

I aim to be gracious and generous (fill in with your commitment to be generous from day 106)

I want to be open-minded (fill in with your commitment to be humble from day 107)

I ask You to give me wisdom to intervene based on Your words: *The godly offer good counsel; they teach right from wrong* (Psalm 37:30 NLT). When I intervene, help me to

Give me the wisdom to encourage others to look to You and Your wisdom in their conflicts. Amen.

SENSE FOR A BIGGER PERSPECTIVE

Please forgive your servant's presumption. The LORD your God will certainly make a lasting dynasty for my lord, because you fight the LORD's battles, and no wrongdoing will be found in you as long as you live. Even though someone is pursuing you to take your life, the life of my lord will be bound securely in the bundle of the living by the LORD your God, but the lives of your enemies he will hurl away as from the pocket of a sling. When the LORD has fulfilled for my lord every good thing he promised concerning him and has appointed him ruler over Israel, my lord will not have on his conscience the staggering burden of needless bloodshed or of having avenged himself. And when the LORD your God has brought my lord success, remember your servant.

1 SAMUEL 25:28–31

Abigail wanted to divert David's attention to more important matters and the bigger picture rather than a petty insult.

Whereas Nabal had said he didn't know David, Abigail knew everything about David.

She knew David was anointed by God to be king. David should not avenge himself because God was with him. God would take revenge. David's life was secure in God's hands—"Even though someone is pursuing you to take your life, the life of my lord will be bound securely in the bundle of the living by the LORD your God" (1 Samuel 25:29). In verse 29, she wisely reminded David of the time he met with Goliath, and the little bag in which David had five stones with the one stone he hurled from his sling to kill Goliath—"but the lives of your enemies he will hurl away as from the pocket of a sling."

David had said when he fought Goliath: "All those gathered here will know that it is not by sword or spear that the LORD saves; for the battle is the LORD's, and he will give all of you into our hands" (17:47).

God had been with David then and given him victory. God would be with David now, and in the future, keeping his life secure. God would win the battles for him. Abigail's argument did not leave David, as a man of God, with any support in taking revenge on Nabal and her household.

Abigail helped David to put events, both human and spiritual, into perspective. She gave him God's perspective, confirming what David already knew but it seems had forgotten in his anger.

There are good reasons why we and others should not seek revenge or aim to avenge ourselves. As Abigail pointed out, it does not make us or others feel better. In fact, it can have the opposite effect, resulting in guilt. It is also pointless and unproductive. It does not solve problems but only allows the avenger to feel powerful and satisfied for a short amount of time.

Most importantly, and from the bigger perspective, it is not what God wants us to do. Let's pray to have wisdom in conflicts to see God's perspective.

Lord God, as I think about my own conflicts and the conflicts of other people, I realize that it is wise to not seek revenge or to avenge myself.

(As you listen to God through the following verses, write down the wisdom you glean in the way you should act in conflicts.) May I always remember that it is instead wise to . . .

"Don't say, 'I will get even for this wrong.' Wait for the LORD to handle the matter" (Proverbs 20:22 NLT). God, help me to

_____

_____ .

"Never pay back evil with more evil. Do things in such a way that everyone can see you are honorable. Do all that you can to live in peace with everyone. Dear friends, never take revenge. Leave that to the righteous anger of God" (Romans 12:17–19 NLT). Give me the wisdom to

_____

_____ .

"Do not seek revenge or bear a grudge against anyone among your people, but love your neighbor as yourself. I am the LORD" (Leviticus 19:18). Lord, teach me

_____

_____ .

"Love your enemies! Do good to them. Lend to them without expecting to be repaid. Then your reward from heaven will be very great, and you will truly be acting as children of the Most High, for he is kind to those who are unthankful and wicked" (Luke 6:35 NLT). Show me

_____

_____ .

"Bless those who persecute you; bless and do not curse" (Romans 12:14). May I

_____

_____ .

I ask for wisdom to help others turn to You and turn their back on taking revenge, that they too can *be bound securely in the bundle of the living by the LORD your God* (1 Samuel 25:29). Amen.

FOR OTHERS TO SEE SENSE

David said to Abigail, "Praise be to the LORD, the God of Israel, who has sent you today to meet me. May you be blessed for your good judgment and for keeping me from bloodshed this day and from avenging myself with my own hands. Otherwise, as surely as the LORD, the God of Israel, lives, who has kept me from harming you, if you had not come quickly to meet me, not one male belonging to Nabal would have been left alive by daybreak." Then David accepted from her hand what she had brought him and said, "Go home in peace. I have heard your words and granted your request."

1 SAMUEL 25:32–35

Abigail had enabled David to see sense—"Praise be to the LORD, the God of Israel, who has sent you today to meet me. May you be blessed for your good judgment and for keeping me from bloodshed this day and from avenging myself with my own hands. . . . Go home in peace," David said to her. "I have heard your words and granted your request" (1 Samuel 25:32–33, 35). The tension was diffused.

Up to that point, Abigail did not know if her actions and words had impacted David. She had acted quickly. She had shown deference. She had sought forgiveness. She had presented David with what he requested. She had spoken wisely. However, she still faced a man who commanded men ready to fight. She did not know if David's fury had subsided.

David's last words had been spoken in rage as a solemn promise before God: "May God strike me and kill me if even one man of his household is still alive tomorrow morning!" (v. 22 NLT). Now only praise came out of David's mouth. Abigail had gotten David to listen to her. His attitude and demeanor had changed. His perspective had been turned around.

David praised Abigail, and David praised God. God had used Abigail's sense to avert disaster and David from taking revenge upon himself. Her good sense had brought to light the folly David was about to commit.

Good sense and wisdom come from God. We need only ask. God-given wisdom does divert disasters and resolve conflicts.

Let's have the confidence and the courage to obey God and intervene prayerfully as we are called, no matter the outcome. Let's be confident that other people will have a change of heart because God has been present and spoken to them through our prayers, words, and actions. When they thank us, we can praise God.

Pray to be a woman who confidently takes the initiative and know that God will work in the conflicts you bring to Him.

Lord God, as I work through conflicts, looking to You for wisdom and discernment when to act and what to say, I will face moments not knowing how the conflicts will be resolved. Yet, I will have confidence that You will be at work.

(As you think about your own conflicts, fill in with your own words of confidence in God.)

I praise You now for what You will do in

_____ .

I praise You for Your wisdom and power to

_____ .

I praise You for giving me the wisdom to

_____ .

I praise You for the peace I have received about

_____ .

Amen.

GOD OF JUSTICE

When Abigail went to Nabal, he was in the house holding a banquet like that of a king. He was in high spirits and very drunk. So she told him nothing at all until daybreak. Then in the morning, when Nabal was sober, his wife told him all these things, and his heart failed him and he became like a stone. About ten days later, the LORD struck Nabal and he died.

1 SAMUEL 25:36–38

Abigail went home to a drunken husband who was totally unaware of the danger averted by his wife. So in her good sense, she didn't speak to Nabal until the next day. Then she told him everything—her decision to give food to David, her encounter with David, the revenge he was about to take on their household, her apology, David's acceptance and decision not to kill their household. The news had a devastating effect on Nabal. God did indeed avenge Nabal for what he had done. David did the right thing in heeding Abigail's wise advice.

We are reminded from Hannah's prayer that God is knowledgeable of the thoughts, words, and actions of each human being. God weighs and repays the deeds of everyone. Even though this can make us afraid, God acts justly and not indiscriminately. God is perfect and so when He brings justice, it is also perfect. Psalm 89:14 tells us that righteousness and justice are the foundation of God's rule over the universe. God does what is right and just. The second part of Psalm 89:14 tells us that steadfast love and faithfulness are part of God's character too. Love and faithfulness are inseparable from His righteousness and justice. We can trust God to act justly.

We do not fear God; instead we do what a righteous and just, loving and faithful God tells us to do: "The LORD has told you what is good, and this is what he requires of you: to do what is right, to love mercy, and to walk humbly with your God" (Micah 6:8 NLT).

Let's pray to be women who do what God requests of us.

Lord God, I am grateful I can trust You to act justly. Thank You that throughout these devotions, I have been learning how to act justly too, to walk humbly with You, and to do what is right. God, I invite You to show me how to live out Micah 6:8 each and every day; teach me more deeply to

act justly (reflect with God how you can *act justly* in your current circumstances and season)

_____

_____

_____ ;

love mercy (reflect with God how you can *love mercy* in your current circumstances and season)

_____

_____

_____ ;

walk humbly before You (reflect with God how you can *walk humbly before Him* in your current circumstances and season)

_____

_____

_____ .

Let me have the confidence to know I am right with You. Amen.

REWARDED

Then David sent word to Abigail, asking her to become his wife.

1 SAMUEL 25:39

At the end of her long speech in the middle of the heat of the conflict, Abigail said these words to David: "And when the LORD your God has brought my lord success, remember your servant" (1 Samuel 25:31).

David remembered Abigail's request.

Abigail's appeal, at the time she met David with the donkeys laden with food, might seem unusual and out of place. What could David possibly do for this woman when they parted ways in that mountain ravine? Maybe Abigail thought there was no harm in asking. Or maybe she knew that David, a man who did what was right, who loved mercy, and walked humbly with God, would repay her kindness with kindness, whatever that might look like.

David did more than remember Abigail; he saved her life. Abigail's marriage to David might seem like the perfect ending to a love story—a beautiful, intelligent woman married to a surly man becomes a widow and is taken to be the wife of the handsome, intelligent man she helped, who one day will be king.

However, more realistically, David's marriage to Abigail saved her, as a widow, from poverty and an uncertain future. We have already discovered with the story of Naomi and Ruth that women in ancient times did not inherit their husband's wealth. David "also married Ahinoam of Jezreel, and they both were his wives" at the same time he married Abigail (v. 43), implying that marriage for a king-in-waiting was more strategic than a love match. However, Abigail's act of kindness toward David was repaid with kindness.

We don't know for sure that the kindness we show other people, the interventions we help with to avert disasters, and the respect we show others in the middle of a conflict will be repaid. But, we can be assured that God takes note of our deeds of kindness.

Let's pray that, when we find ourselves in need, the same generosity, forgiveness, patience, and kindness we have shown others will be shown to us.

Lord God, thank You for the power of kindness. I ask You to show me kindness by

_____

_____

_____ .

Even though I don't give kindness just so I will be shown kindness, I do ask that when and where I need the kindness of other people, that they will be there for me.

I ask that I will experience generosity in the form of

_____ .

I ask that I will be forgiven for

_____ .

I ask that I will be shown patience when

_____ .

I ask that I will be treated with gentleness by

_____ .

Most of all, I thank You for Your generosity, forgiveness, patience, and gentleness shown to me. Amen.

A WOMAN WITH PURPOSE
Esther

Esther, a Jewish woman, lived in Susa in the Persian Empire as an exile. She was an orphan raised by her cousin Mordecai. King Xerxes of Persia selected Esther to be his queen.

Esther's story stands in contrast to the stories of the other women we have looked at so far in that there is no mention of God or faith in her story. Yet, Esther is seen as a woman of piety and duty who uses enormous courage to bring about God's purpose in saving the Jewish people from annihilation. We can learn from Esther how we too can be devoted to God's purposes in environments and situations where God is not visible in people's lives.

WINNING FAVOR

And Esther won the favor of everyone who saw her. . . . Now the king was attracted to Esther more than to any of the other women, and she won his favor and approval more than any of the other virgins. So he set a royal crown on her head and made her queen instead of Vashti.

ESTHER 2:15, 17

K ing Xerxes crowned an ordinary woman from an insignificant family as his queen. Esther, a Jewish captive in exile, became the most notable woman in the Persian Empire.

As Esther rose to be queen, Esther gained popularity with all who came in contact with her in the palace. Everyone thought well of her. In particular, Esther's exemplary behavior and attitude caught the attention of Hegai, the eunuch in charge of the harem, who singled her out as a likely candidate for the position of queen.[a] Esther received preferential treatment from Hegai.[b]

Most importantly, Esther won the "favor" of the king (Esther 2:17). The word *favor* is the same Hebrew word, *hesed*, we have encountered in the stories of Rahab and Ruth. It encompasses words such as "kindness," "loyalty," and "goodwill." Esther won all of these qualities from the king.

From entering the palace to being selected as queen, Esther conducted herself well.

[a] When the turn came for Esther (the young woman Mordecai had adopted, the daughter of his uncle Abihail) to go to the king, she asked for nothing other than what Hegai, the king's eunuch who was in charge of the harem, suggested. And Esther won the favor of everyone who saw her (Esther 2:15).

[b] Read Esther 2:8–9.

293

Esther, a young Jewish orphan, probably never imagined she would be alongside the most important man of the Persian Empire.

Although we are unlikely to be crowned as royalty, we too may end up in circumstances different than we imagined or planned. Wherever we find ourselves, we should aim to be exceptional in our behaviors and impeccable in our attitudes toward everyone and every situation. We should aim to be women who God has created us to be, reflecting His image.

Let's pray to be women who conduct ourselves well so that those around us look upon us favorably, and that we win their kindness, loyalty, and goodwill.

Lord God, these are the circumstances I find myself in that are different than I imagined or planned:

_____

_____

_____ .

These are the people who surround me in these places:

_____

_____

_____ .

Even though I am an ordinary woman, I want my conduct to be exemplary in all circumstances and with all people. Give me the sense and strength to have an attitude of compassion, kindness, gentleness, patience, even-temperedness, forgiveness, humility, honesty, sensitivity, thoughtfulness.[a] (Choose one of these attributes you need to work on, or a

[a] Based on Colossians 3:8–9, 12–13.

different one that comes to mind, and ask God to show you how you can improve.) Help me to

_____

_____ .

Forgive me for

_____

_____ .

Amen.

FACING FEAR

Then she [Esther] instructed him to say to Mordecai, "All the king's officials and the people of the royal provinces know that for any man or woman who approaches the king in the inner court without being summoned the king has but one law: that they be put to death unless the king extends the gold scepter to them and spares their lives. But thirty days have passed since I was called to go to the king."

ESTHER 4:10–11

Esther learned from Mordecai that Haman, the king's most trusted advisor with significant power, had decreed a ruling in the Persian Empire to "destroy, kill and annihilate all the Jews—young and old, women and children—on a single day" (Esther 3:13).

Mordecai instructed Esther "to go into the king's presence to beg for mercy and plead with him for her people" (Esther 4:8). However, Esther's courage faltered when she received this instruction, and with good reason. If Esther went into the king's presence uninvited, she faced the severest of consequences—death. No matter how she had charmed and delighted the king since he made her queen, Xerxes's favoritism could not be guaranteed. Any approach by Esther was fraught with risk, particularly because she had not been invited into the king's presence for one whole month. Not only that, but Esther had not revealed her Jewish identity.

Esther's task seemed impossible. Her fear justified.

We don't have to be in a life-or-death situation for our courage to falter. Anything that is a threat to our credibility, livelihoods, or relationships can seem daunting. Maybe you don't often talk about or reveal your faith because of the fear of ridicule or disapproval. Perhaps you fear the consequences of losing your job if you speak out about what is unethical at work. Maybe you agree to what is unacceptable at home for fear of disrupting the peace. Even when someone points out the greater good we can do, we can still hesitate because the consequences for ourselves are overwhelming.

Pray about the fears you have of speaking up for what is right and good, especially when the negative consequences for yourself are real.

Lord God, these are the challenging situations I face in which I need courage:

_____

_____

_____ .

This is what I sense I need to do (write down the ways in which you should speak or act):

_____

_____

_____ .

These are the consequences, real and imagined, that I struggle with:

_____

_____ .

I have to admit that fear can get the better of me. Help me overcome my fear. Amen.

FAITH OVER FEAR

When Esther's words were reported to Mordecai, he sent back this answer: "Do not think that because you are in the king's house you alone of all the Jews will escape. For if you remain silent at this time, relief and deliverance for the Jews will arise from another place, but you and your father's family will perish. And who knows but that you have come to your royal position for such a time as this?"

ESTHER 4:12–14

If Esther went before the king uninvited, she could lose her life. If she did nothing, she could still lose her life. Whatever way she wanted to protect her life, she could lose it anyway.

In Esther 4:12–14, Mordecai's words to Esther implied that God would find a way to save His people. God could accomplish His plan without Esther. God didn't need Esther to save lives, but Esther needed God to save her life. Esther could choose to have God accomplish His plan through her and step into the role that Mordecai believed God had for her.

Esther, however, faced a dilemma. She could give in to fear, or she could have faith in God.

Mordecai's question to Esther was to encourage her to consider that God had placed her in the palace for His purposes. But, Esther needed to build up her faith so it was greater than her fear to step into God's purposes.

Perhaps in your own life, you can see that you have more fear than faith. God has a purpose for each of us in the places we find ourselves. Sometimes those places are challenging and godless. Sometimes they are frightening and risky. Other times they are comfortable and easy. The challenge for each of us, whatever our situation, is to choose faith over fear of standing out, losing out, or giving up our comforts.

Most of us want to step into the purposes God has for us. But, when the task God has assigned for us is full of personal risk, it is normal to falter.

Let's pray to trust God with our lives. Let's pray to be women who step up our commitment to God in fulfilling His purposes, and not step away from deciding to follow Him and His ways. Tell God about your fear in the situation that is *for such a time as this.*

Lord God, I am not as brave as I'd like to be. I am tempted to give in to my fears of

_____

_____ .

I will hold onto the many reassurances You give in Your Word that tell me I do not need to be afraid. (Fill in the blanks with your name.)

"Do not be afraid, _____ , for I will protect you, and your reward will be great" (Genesis 15:1 NLT).

"Do not be afraid, _____ ; be glad and rejoice. Surely the LORD has done great things!" (Joel 2:21).

"This is what the LORD says—he who made you, who formed you in the womb, and who will help you: Do not be afraid, _____ , whom I have chosen" (Isaiah 44:2).

"What is the matter, _____ ? Do not be afraid; God has heard" (Genesis 21:17).

"And you, _____ , do not be afraid of them or their words" (Ezekiel 2:6).

Lord, give me the strength to choose faith over fear, to step up instead of step away, to be useful to You and not overlooked by You. Amen.

TAKING CHARGE

> Then Esther sent this reply to Mordecai: "Go, gather together all the Jews who are in Susa, and fast for me. Do not eat or drink for three days, night or day. I and my attendants will fast as you do. When this is done, I will go to the king, even though it is against the law. And if I perish, I perish."
>
> ESTHER 4:15–16

Esther decided to step up to the challenge presented to her by Mordecai. She would bravely go before the king even if she lost her life. But, she would not do this alone.

Esther engaged the support of two groups of people to come alongside her. One, the wider community of people whose lives were impacted by the decree and who were invested in the outcome of her task. These were Jews who were already fasting.[a] Two, a small group of people who were closest to her and knew the day-to-day details of her life. These were people who already looked upon her favorably and with whom she could trust to reveal her identity of being Jewish.

Esther would ask the Jewish people to fast. In the Old Testament, fasting often took place in times of emergency, when people needed God to deliver them from disaster. People also fasted to secure God's help and guidance. And fasting usually included prayer.[1]

Esther took charge, and she took on responsibility for the task ahead of her. She did not rush before the king even though the decree created a dire situation for her people.

[a] In every province to which the edict and order of the king came, there was great mourning among the Jews, with fasting, weeping and wailing. Many lay in sackcloth and ashes (Esther 4:3).

She took time with those who supported her through prayer and fasting to build up her faith in God.

With Esther, we can see how to move forward into God's purposes that we find difficult and fearful. On one hand, we step out alone in faith. We make the decision to step into God's purposes. No one can do that for us. On the other hand, we do not have to step out alone. We ask our community to join us in powerfully petitioning God for His protection, help, and guidance. In doing so, God is with us.

We too can ask a wider community of people who are invested in God's purposes for us to pray and fast for us. And we can bring on board a few close confidants, those who especially like us.

We do not face God's plans and purposes alone. We do everything we can with everyone who can join us. As you step into God's purposes, think about the people you can ask to be your support *for such a time as this*. Add them to your prayer below.

Lord God, when I make the decision to step into the purposes You have for me. I do this boldly, but not alone. I ask that (identify intercessors from Day 92 who can pray for you and support you)

_____

_____

_____

will come alongside me, pray for me, and even fast for me. May these people build up my faith and trust in You. Amen.

ACTION THAT IS FAVORABLE

On the third day Esther put on her royal robes and stood in the inner court of the palace, in front of the king's hall. The king was sitting on his royal throne in the hall, facing the entrance. When he saw Queen Esther standing in the court, he was pleased with her and held out to her the gold scepter that was in his hand. So Esther approached and touched the tip of the scepter. Then the king asked, "What is it, Queen Esther? What is your request? Even up to half the kingdom, it will be given you."

ESTHER 5:1–3

The moment had arrived like stepping onto a stage, but much worse. Esther stood in the inner court, visible to the king. By doing so, Esther had already broken the law by coming before the king uninvited.[a]

In that moment, she did not know how the king would respond. The king, however, was "pleased with her" (Esther 5:2). Even more than finding pleasure at her appearance, the king looked on her with favor. He showed grace in accepting and forgiving her for coming to him uninvited. He showed kindness and generosity in offering her "up to half the kingdom" (v. 3).

Esther's task had appeared so terrifying and difficult, but the outcome was so delightful and straightforward.

Esther, however, had done everything she could to make the outcome favorable. She had put on her royal gowns

[a] "The two words 'and stood' must not be overlooked (Esther 5:1). This was an act of breaking the law by standing in the king's court without having been called. Esther had come to her moment of truth. She publicly had confronted the king."[2]

and used the formal language expected on such an occasion before a king. She had approached the king correctly and respectfully as expected in her role as queen. Esther had made the environment as beneficial as she could for success.

Esther and the people had fasted and sought God's protection in preparation for this occasion. And God had prepared a king who would look favorably upon Esther. He had opened the way for Esther to make her request for reversing an edict made by two of the most powerful men in the Persian Empire.

When we step out in faith to do God's purposes, we can trust God will make conditions favorable for us. We petition and trust that God will go ahead of us to prepare the way. At the same time, we do everything in our capacity to make conditions as favorable as we can.

As you step into what God has planned for you, do so believing that with the foundation of prayer you have built, God has prepared the way for you. Pray also for the wisdom to do everything you can on your part to bring about God's purposes.

Lord God, I commit to stepping out for You where and when needed. I am trusting You to go ahead of me and prepare the way. (Read God's words in the verses below spoken to you, then for one or more of them, thank God and write how You will trust Him.)

"Do not be afraid or discouraged, for the LORD will personally go ahead of you. He will be with you; he will neither fail you nor abandon you" (Deuteronomy 31:8 NLT). Thank You for

_____ .

I trust You to

_____ .

"See, I am sending an angel ahead of you to guard you along the way and to bring you to the place I have prepared" (Exodus 23:20). Thank You for

_____ .

I trust You to

_____ .

"You hem me in behind and before, and you lay your hand upon me" (Psalm 139:5). Thank You for

_____ .

I trust You to

_____ .

"Your word is a lamp for my feet, a light on my path" (Psalm 119:105). Thank You for

_____ .

I trust You to

_____ .

"I will go before you and will level the mountains; I will break down gates of bronze and cut through bars of iron" (Isaiah 45:2). Thank You for

_____ .

I trust You to

_____ .

Amen.

HAVING DISCERNMENT

Then Queen Esther answered, "If I have found favor with you, Your Majesty, and if it pleases you, grant me my life—this is my petition. And spare my people—this is my request. For I and my people have been sold to be destroyed, killed and annihilated. If we had merely been sold as male and female slaves, I would have kept quiet, because no such distress would justify disturbing the king.

ESTHER 7:3–4

Three times the king said to Esther, "What is your request? Even up to half the kingdom, it will be granted" (Esther 5:3; 5:6; 7:2). The first time the king asked his question and offered her half the kingdom was when Esther stood before the king in the court. The second time was when Esther invited the king and Haman to a banquet. On the third occasion when the king and Haman went to Esther's banquet, Esther was ready to give her answer.

If Esther was waiting for reassurance that her request would be accepted, she had it. The king, however, was expecting Esther to ask for wealth and power, not her life. It would most likely have been a surprise to the king when he realized Esther was asking him to "grant me my life" (Esther 7:3)—to spare her from death.

On each occasion the king asked to know her request, Esther pleaded with the king to be pleased with her, and to respond favorably toward her. She would need the king's utmost goodwill for what she was asking. She wanted him to overturn a decree that he had signed, an agreement to kill his own wife and queen. The king was not a man who liked to be made to look foolish.

Esther did not rush, though, in answering the king's question. She showed respect for the king and behaved within the customs and etiquette expected

[a] "Conversation and preparation are essential in any important transaction."[3]

of Middle Eastern protocol at that time.[a] Esther displayed tact, wisdom, and discernment.

When we are in a place ordained by God *for such a time as this*, we too should conduct ourselves with as much understanding and wisdom as we can. Even though we have faith in God's leading and trust Him for the outcome, we do not go into situations without perception and understanding. We use the minds God has given us to the best of our ability, and we use the wisdom He has given us.

Wisdom begins with reverence and respect for God. Esther had already begun her task with reverence for God, by spending three days pleading for God's protection and seeking His guidance. Likewise, our starting point should always be to spend time with God, but we should not be afraid to use our intellect and understanding.

Let's be women who always seek God first but use the minds God has given us to make good and wise decisions as we carry out God's purposes.

Lord God, throughout these devotions, I have committed to seeking You in all I do. I have prayed to understand and grow in wisdom, to have faith over fear, for You to go ahead of me, for humility (fill in with other ways you have learned to pray),

_____

_____

_____

_____

_____

_____

_____

I have committed to trusting You in all that I do (fill in with some of your circumstances you have committed to God), including

_____

_____

_____

_____

_____ .

Now, I commit to using the mind you have given me, as a woman created in Your image and likeness and as an *ezer*, to discern the way forward in all areas of my life. Amen.

GOD-GIVEN AUTHORITY

Esther again pleaded with the king, falling at his feet and weeping. . . .
"If it pleases the king," she said, "and if he regards me with favor and
thinks it the right thing to do, and if he is pleased with me, let an order
be written overruling the dispatches that Haman son of Hammedatha,
the Agagite, devised and wrote to destroy the Jews in all the king's
provinces. For how can I bear to see disaster fall on my people? How
can I bear to see the destruction of my family?"

ESTHER 8:3, 5–6

Esther succeeded in bringing to the king's attention the edict that would
result in the loss of her life and the death of all the Jews in Persia. She
succeeded in having Haman, the king's most trusted adviser, who had significant power and was an enemy of the Jews, removed from power and
from being a further threat to the Jewish people.

Esther received from the king the wealth of Haman's estate, and Mordecai
was established into the king's court. Esther's position had been elevated,
her life and Mordecai's life had been saved. Esther could have stopped
there. But, there was more to be done. The decree needed to be overturned.

Esther needed the king's favor one more time. This time, Esther didn't
stand in her royal robes before the king nor use the formal language expected on such an occasion. Instead she pleaded and wept, falling at his
feet in an undignified manner.

It could have been that Esther had found new courage from her success
in receiving the king's favor so far. As Haman, the king's powerful adviser,
was no longer a threat and with Mordecai at the king's side, Esther could
have felt braver. It could have been that the annihilation of a large group
of people required a more passionate approach. Esther's difference in approach could have been for all three reasons. Whichever it was, Esther had
become bolder in petitioning the king.

When we see God at work, we too become bolder. When we see outcomes that reassure us God is in control, it gives us greater courage. When God prepares the way, we can keep going unafraid.

Where have you seen God at work in your life? Think about the times God has been with you, going in front of you and answering your prayers. Then pray to become bolder and more courageous in continuing the plan God has for you.

Lord God, thank You for the times You have been with me, going before me and answering my prayers. Thank You for the times I have seen You at work in my life:

_____

_____

Thank You for how and where I have seen You at work in the circumstances I have prayed about throughout these devotions:

_____

_____

Never let me forget what You have done for me. I ask that in remembering what You have done so far, I will become bolder and more courageous in moving forward and in doing my part in Your plans and purposes. (Write down ways in which you are being invited by God to be bolder.)

_____

_____

_____

Amen.

STEPPING INTO GOD'S PURPOSES

So Queen Esther, daughter of Abihail, along with Mordecai the Jew, wrote with full authority to confirm this second letter concerning Purim. And Mordecai sent letters to all the Jews in the 127 provinces of Xerxes' kingdom—words of goodwill and assurance—to establish these days of Purim at their designated times, as Mordecai the Jew and Queen Esther had decreed for them, and as they had established for themselves and their descendants in regard to their times of fasting and lamentation. Esther's decree confirmed these regulations about Purim, and it was written down in the records.

ESTHER 9:29–32

Esther began as a young, unknown Jewish woman in the king's harem to becoming a diplomat, making decisions on behalf of the king. A decree could not be overturned, but a new order could be written to overrule the decree. And for this, Esther had the king's approval to write it. Esther used the authority she had been given by the king to establish a new Persian law.

What Mordecai persuaded her to do, what he had pointed out to her about her position was true. She had assurance that she was in this position as queen *for such a time as this*. However, it was not to just save her own skin but all her people.

Esther started out unsure that she could have any impact on the king or on the rulings made by the two most powerful men in the Persian Empire. Yet throughout, Esther has found favor with the king. Esther had done her part well.

We must not underestimate what God can do when we are willing to step out, do our part, and risk everything for him. But we do not do so without preparation.

So far, you have prayed to find favor and be shown favor. You have learned to prepare through prayer and fasting. You know to have faith instead of fear. With God on our side, our fears are unfounded. Now wait to see what God can do with your obedience, and then marvel when you see Him at work.

Lord God, I am eager to be used for Your plans and purposes. Help me remember that I do so seeking Your favor and the favor of others. I will also remember the importance of doing so with a firm foundation of prayer—my own prayers and the prayers of others. (With God, reflect on the lessons you've learned about prayer during this 120-day journey.)

(Reflect on three ways you want to put those lessons about prayer into practice in the coming weeks.)

_____

_____

_____

_____

_____

_____

_____

_____

_____

_____

_____

_____

_____

_____

_____

_____

_____

_____

I look forward to marveling at You at work. Amen.

ACKNOWLEDGMENTS

My heartfelt thanks to the wonderful team at Our Daily Bread Publishing. In particular, I am grateful to Dawn Anderson for bringing this project to life. I have been blessed with amazing editors, Anna Haggard and JR Hudberg. Thank you for making me think more clearly and clarifying my thoughts on paper. It's been a delight working with you. Thank you also to the Our Daily Bread Publishing team for the kindness and patience shown to me when I had emergency surgery for appendicitis while in the middle of working on my edits.

To my agent, Barb Roose at Books & Such Literary Agency, it is an absolute pleasure working with you. I love the ease and style you bring to our working relationship. Thank you for your expertise and professionalism. I value the direction in which you point me.

Thank you to my husband, Colin, who is my greatest supporter, my technical guru when I need to focus on tapping out words on the laptop, my chef, my tea maker, and so much more. I love how you care for me, and I love you.

To my children, Phoebe, George, and Maximilian, you are the best. Thank you for giving me confidence and being great believers in my abilities as an author. The few words with which I thank you here are nothing compared to the immensity of thankfulness in my heart for having you as my children. It's such fun doing life with you.

To my extended family and friends across the pond in England, thank you for always showing an interest in my work. To my aunt and uncle, Christine and Trevor Ransome, thank you for being excited about my contract with Our Daily Bread Publishing, and most of all for praying for me. You have stepped into the void of my parents' passing. When I wanted to enthuse about this book to Mum and Dad, you took their place and showed enthusiasm in return.

I am grateful for my author friends here in the States, especially Cynthia Fantasia and the late Lucinda Secrest McDowell, who have encouraged and praised my writing and played a part in making this book possible. To the Keeping Buoyant women, especially Patty MacDonald, and the reNEW community of writers and speakers—you are an important part of being on this journey with me. Then there are my many non-author friends and friends who do not share the same faith as me. Thank you for being wonderfully open, generous, and kindhearted. My prayer is that you will experience a new dimension to life through this book.

Lastly, but in no way least, I am grateful to my heavenly Father for His loving patience with me. He planted in my heart the excitement and deep-down fulfillment that comes from a relationship with Him, and from hearing Him say, "Rachel, talk to Me . . ."

NOTES

A woman of hope: Practicing prayer from the life of Eve

1. T. C. Mitchell, "In the Old Testament," in *New Bible Dictionary*, ed. D. R. W. Wood et al. (Leicester, England; Downers Grove, IL: InterVarsity Press, 1996), 13.
2. Robert Jamieson, A. R. Fausset, and David Brown, *Commentary Critical and Explanatory on the Whole Bible*, vol. 1 (Oak Harbor, WA: Logos Research Systems, Inc., 1997), 19.
3. K. A. Mathews, ed., *The New American Commentary*, vol. 1A, *Genesis 1–11:26* (Nashville: Broadman & Holman Publishers, 1996), 254.

A woman on a journey of faith: Practicing prayer from the life of Sarah

1. K. A. Mathews, ed., *The New American Commentary*, vol. 1B, *Genesis 11:27–50:26* (Nashville: Broadman & Holman Publishers, 2005), 218–219.

A woman who experienced God's presence: Practicing prayer from the life of Hagar

1. K. A. Mathews, ed., *The New American Commentary*, vol. 1B, *Genesis 11:27–50:26* (Nashville: Broadman & Holman Publishers, 2005), 189.

An overenthusiastic woman: Practicing prayer from the life of Rebekah

1. William David Reyburn and Euan McG. Fry, *A Handbook on Genesis* (New York: United Bible Societies, 1998), 586.

A woman of sorrow: Practicing prayer from the life of Rachel
A woman overlooked: Practicing prayer from the life of Leah

1. Chad Brand et al., eds., "Gad," in *Holman Illustrated Bible Dictionary* (Nashville: Holman Bible Publishers, 2003), 610.
2. Stelman Smith and Judson Cornwall, "Asher," *The Exhaustive Dictionary of Bible Names* (North Brunswick, NJ: Bridge-Logos, 1998), 23.
3. K. A. Mathews, ed., *The New American Commentary*, vol. 1B, *Genesis 11:27–50:26* (Nashville: Broadman & Holman Publishers, 2005), 486.
4. Patricia L. Crawford and Mark Allan Powell, "Mandrake," in *The HarperCollins Bible Dictionary (Revised and Updated)*, ed. Mark Allan Powell (New York: HarperCollins, 2011), 595.
5. Walter A. Elwell and Barry J. Beitzel, "Ben-Oni," in *Baker Encyclopedia of the Bible* (Grand Rapids, MI: Baker Book House, 1988), 282.

A woman learning humility: Practicing prayer from the life of Miriam

1. Douglas K. Stuart, *The New American Commentary*, vol. 2, *Exodus* (Nashville: Broadman & Holman Publishers, 2006), 346.

A woman with many roles: Practicing prayer from the life of Deborah

1. Simon J Robinson, *Opening up Judges* (Leominster: Day One Publications, 2006), 28.

A woman of tragedy: Practicing prayer from the life of Naomi

1. M. G. Easton, *Illustrated Bible Dictionary and Treasury of Biblical History, Biography, Geography, Doctrine, and Literature* (New York: Harper & Brothers, 1893), 309.
2. Chad Brand et al., eds., "Naomi," in *Holman Illustrated Bible Dictionary* (Nashville: Holman Bible Publishers, 2003), 1174.

3. Daniel Isaac Block, *The New American Commentary*, vol. 6, *Judges, Ruth* (Nashville: Broadman & Holman Publishers, 1999), 670.

A woman under God's wings: Practicing prayer from the life of Ruth

1. Daniel Isaac Block, *The New American Commentary*, vol. 6, *Judges, Ruth* (Nashville: Broadman & Holman Publishers, 1999), 721–722.

A woman of strength: Practicing prayer from the life of Hannah

1. Robert D. Bergen, ed., *The New American Commentary*, vol. 7, *1, 2 Samuel* (Nashville: Broadman & Holman Publishers, 1996), 70.

A woman with purpose: Practicing prayer from the life of Esther

1. Clarence B. Bass, "Fast, Fasting," in *Baker Encyclopedia of the Bible* (Grand Rapids, MI: Baker Book House, 1988), 780; H. A. G. Belben, "Fasting," in *New Bible Dictionary*, ed. D. R. W. Wood et al. (Leicester, England; Downers Grove, IL: InterVarsity Press, 1996), 364; Roger L. Omanson and Philip A. Noss, *A Handbook on the Book of Esther: The Hebrew and Greek Texts* (New York: United Bible Societies, 1997), 133.
2. Mervin Breneman, *The New American Commentary*, vol. 10, *Ezra, Nehemiah, Esther* (Nashville: Broadman & Holman Publishers, 1993), 339.
3. Breneman, *New American Commentary*, 10:340.

GOD HEARS HER.

Seek and she will find

Spread the Word
by Doing One Thing.

- Give a copy of this book as a gift.
- Share the QR code link via your social media.
- Write a review of this book on your blog, favorite bookseller's website, or at ODB.org/store.
- Recommend this book to your church, small group, or book club.

Connect with us. 🅵 🅾

Our Daily Bread Publishing
PO Box 3566, Grand Rapids, MI 49501, USA
Email: books@odb.org

Love God. Love Others.

with  Our Daily Bread®

Your gift changes lives.

Connect with us. 🅕 🄾

Our Daily Bread Publishing
PO Box 3566, Grand Rapids, MI 49501, USA
Email: books@odb.org